THENEW CENSUS an ANTHOLOGY of CONTEMPORARY AMERICAN POETRY

RESCUE PRESS
CHICAGO, CLEVELAND, IOWA CITY

Copyright © 2013
All rights reserved
Printed in the United States of America
First Edition
ISBN 978-0-9885873-1-1

Design by Sevy Perez
Illustrations by Lauren Haldeman
In Brandon Grotesque OT and Tisa OT
rescuepress.co

THE NEW CENSUS

an ANTHOLOGY of CONTEMPORARY AMERICAN POETRY

Edited by Kevin A. González & Lauren Shapiro

FOREWORD

To take in something new, to be given some things one's not before encountered. This is one way our lives galvanize, one way we keep salt salty. Encountering the assembled poets in *The New Census* first of all attracts eye, ear, mind, heart, soul, whatever you call our life-fuel, whatever it is one wants to keep up and running.

Demographics aside, what all these poets have in common is will, is faithfulness to poetry's multiplicities, is some kind, manifest as many kinds, of tenacious tending to those powerful places a page of poetry sets before us. Before one word is read, before a line—if there are lines of the traditional kind—resolves itself toward another line, before syntax keeps it all together (and leans us one way or another) (and registers tones and moods and facts and figures), before almost anything has happened, poetry waits there, and we know it is there. It's almost as if a reader is a burning matchhead, about to touch a poem, resulting in lighting it on fire.

We encounter poetry differently. We are in need of different kinds of poetry. It enters our heads differently. It enters our heads and it stays there and it does something to us, sometimes with us, sometimes for us.

Poems gathered here have this in common: they are interesting, that is they are the opposite of boring, they collectively behave as though it is their duty to attract our attention, and then do something with it, something valuable, something useful, something necessary for a spirit's survival.

We're meeting these poets just as they've begun to go on their ways, they've almost all published at least two, no more than three or four collections. It's a crucial time in an artist's story. She's arrived on the scene, someone has noticed, now she's at a crossroads. Where will she go? The original spirit one brings to one's earliest work needs to be acknowledged, possibly found again, possibly over and over again, if one is to continue. These poets have crossed over from private to public, they've sacrificed their privacy, they no longer keep their delicious secrets to themselves.

I don't think anyone (not anyone with an ounce of sense anyway) presumes to feel what Rimbaud felt when he abandoned poetry for adventure. We glorify him though. We treat him as if, what—as if what he's done is heroic. I wonder why. It feels right that we do.

It's true that sometimes what we think we already know keeps us from seeing something fabulous and wonderful. What we know can obscure what we've never encountered before. The editors of *The New Census* have taken care to present to us what's new. It is coming over the horizon, toward us, to give us something, to alert us.

More people are writing and reading poetry on this planet than have ever before. We might as well call it Planet Poetry for all the bristling waves of poetry we sense circulating around the world.

Dara Wier

THE NEW
CENSUS
an ANTHOLOGY of CONTEMPORARY AMERICAN POETRY

Edited by Kevin A. González & Lauren Shapiro

INTRODUCTION

When the publishers of Rescue Press approached us about editing a new anthology of contemporary American poetry, we were thrilled. Though there are a number of wonderful poetry anthologies available, we felt that there was room still for a collection composed of writers in the earlier stages of their careers: writers who, in the last decade or so, have inspired, complicated, and transformed our sense of poetry and poetry's possibilities. Such a collection would appeal to writers and readers of poetry, certainly, but we also imagined the anthology as the start of a conversation about writing, reading, form, content, context, and practice between teachers and students. Having taught creative writing classes (and recalling our own first experiences encountering poets who moved us), we sought to create a new census of sorts, to gather work that would represent a small but electrifying portion of contemporary American poetry. To that end, we hope that the pages you now hold in your hands act as a great first taste of what is out there, as something that might be tucked under the arm while riding the train or spotted askance on the floor of a dorm room. We hope to find this book wrinkled and bent in the library, lent to a new friend, and scarred by the marks of a reader's pen. We hope, too, that *The New Census* is not just useful but that it also serves as the start of a long and winding fall down the remarkable rabbit-hole that is poetry.

The task of selecting writers to include in an anthology can be tricky business, mainly because a book is a finite form and the combinations of writers and material that could be included in it are infinite. The many iterations this book could have taken both invigorated and terrified us, but ultimately we knew we would arrive at only one. During the selection process we read hundreds of books, many by authors we had never read before. We also relied on the advice of friends, fellow poets, and the editors of Rescue Press, with the result that some of the poets in the anthology were new to us. These conversations were part of the fun. The overarching strategy was to include authors who we believe are at the (relative) beginning of enduring poetic careers and to choose work that represents diverse styles and subject matter; we wanted to showcase a wide range of approaches to poetry. There are thus narrative poems alongside more experimental work and poets tackling issues of race and sexual orientation alongside those exploring the more esoteric intricacies of language on the page. There is humor, banality, and gravity; there is an awareness of formal considerations and a rejection of them. We cast a wide net, but of course our selections must necessarily reflect our own biases as readers. As part of the anthology you will also find, side by side with the poems, anonymous answers by our authors to a series of questions about influence, inspiration, and incidentals as a way of providing a bit of interesting and time-sensitive context. We hope that you enjoy the work that you are about to read; the state of poetry in America is strong, and if these voices are any indication, the future looks bright.

Kevin A. González & Lauren Shapiro, Editors

CARRIE OLIVIA ADAMS
lives in Chicago where she works as a book publicist and as the poetry editor for the small press Black Ocean. She is the author of *Intervening Absence* (Ahsahta Press, 2009) and *Forty-One Jane Doe's* (Ahsahta Press, 2013), which includes a DVD of her poem films. Her poems and films have have appeared in such journals as *Cannibal, DIAGRAM, Horse Less, Thermos, Laurel Review, Slope,* and *Dear Camera.*

NOTES TOWARD A SHORT FILM

First only gray,

then angles and points become a whole.

A gravel driveway.

This scene is set
on the road in front,

so as the driveway comes into view, move

to the left of the frame
to foreground her face.
No,

just the eyes and above.

What she would like:

To be living every scene at once

The conversation should be on the balcony.
But the camera is inside the room.
We witness it only through the glass panes of the door.
The lighting crisp. The sky as if about to crack.

We are not watching faces, but his shirt flaps blowing.
He looks away from the camera and over the balcony railing.
Though facing him, she will tell him without ever looking up.

But maybe this is a silent film.

And all that could be told will be spoken
by her hand as it repetitively traces the inside
of her forearm. Maybe we see
only her fingers.

What he doesn't know:

The window is open

If she were to speak—

What I want to know is:
How much have I made up? What is real in the real of you?

If I said cleave:
I meant flung. The parabola. The pronunciation of.

And when I said this is a note to be taped to the underside of your elbow

I meant:
Knee, or maybe shin, or maybe I forgot who I was talking to.

When I said here take this
it's a piece of me
and you held out your hands
as if waiting for a box

Did you know:
The offer was the piece?

A thresher sits off screen.
A yellow halo from the sun.
They make gestures in its direction.
But never at it. They never see it.

Later, in a field
the camera films only their outlines.
Its real interest is the bent and matted blades
of grass their footsteps leave behind.

Her hair blows across the lens

Even the accidentals will remain

This itself was unexpected

**ERIC
BAUS**

is the author of four
books of poetry, *The
Tranquilized Tongue*
(City Lights, 2014),
Scared Text, selected
by Cole Swensen for
the Colorado Prize
(Colorado State
University Press,
2011), *Tuned Droves*
(Octopus Books,
2009), and *The To
Sound*, selected by
Forrest Gander for
the Verse Prize and
recipient of the
Greenwall Fund
of the Academy of
American Poets
(Verse Press/Wave
Books, 2004). He
lives and teaches
in Denver.

THE TO SOUND

To look out a window is to want to be on the side of the birds.

You arrange your arms so the distance is clear.

If the entire was wound. Breathed glass. A tooth embedded so far it burst.

A cut of your cloth to negate every saw.

You are the one after zero. The sister of a. Bird tuned to ash.

To pronounce your medicine in my mouth.

I know I can never understand the. Even if the was powder on my lips.

Unacknowledged and disguised as *O Zero, et tu?*

If my eye could stay glass. Breathe. And stem.

Can a wound enter the was? Can one entire turn?

Stay. I know the tired sound.

To look out a window is to be embedded inside birds.

If I could amplify your glass. Atone for the sound of my incessant lips.

You are a. Too. Tuned to has. Ash.

You are the you and. The to sound. The utter the.

If I have to spit out all my teeth to stay in the.

The. Is it all to say the weight of the?

If I could stay lost to sound. If a single eye could say two.

To breathe glass. To unwind a wing.

To say the entire wound as window. Stone turned to sound.

If the sting unwound itself as sleet. As rain in the cut stem.

If the window to pronounce magnifies.

You are the one after end. The burned bird I woke up in.

WONDERING WHY HER SKIN FEELS LIKE SAND

the accomplished alchemist becomes blue scales on the belly of a sturgeon trapped in the waves of the Mediterranean Sea. Becomes aluminum under the gold plating of two spoons crossed in the open casket of a quail's egg. Becomes the sweetness of milk dissolved in an injured physician's cup of coffee.

She hides in the long wet hairs of his black handlebar mustache. Escapes into the air when he coughs a cough of black smoke into the air. Flushed like a goose stumbled into flight. Flecked with buckshot.

He is clenched for revenge after lifetimes of stifled rage. He is in hate with the parentheses around his left fist. He is a sporting man, with a belly full of scrambled eggs and breath as thick as butter, night, blood.

Of course she runs into the streets where the black stones are passing out. Of course she finds a blind corner, pauses to think of x-ray machines and calculators that conspire against her in laboratories before bringing a plumed bottle of water up to the hole in her chest.

She can feel the row of fluorescent lights in her spine. She can feel a handful of sugar suffering in water.

The physician is twenty stethoscopes away and closing with two rusty spoons nearly crossed into an x.

Suddenly her water becomes unfair. Breaks simply in the bodies around him. Suddenly becomes unfair. Leaves a pile of rotten caviar. A shoeful of sucrose. A single peacock feather riddled with lice. A fisherman swoons poisoned by tainted poultry. The physician draws an x in the rubble with a knuckle from his right hand. Fishes for a ghost until dawn. But the alchemist is accomplished. Her grains scattered by his heavy breath.

Twenty blocks away a little girl throws a firecracker at the feet of a little boy. Gold sparks burning the short blond hairs of his legs.

ORGANS OF THE PROJECTOR

When the phone rings a man appears. His song rings and I am suddenly speaking to the true sun soloist. He is being a perfect listener or a void the perfect listener has stirred.

The organs of the projector are simple for him: "My statue has amplified its lungs." Without opening his eyes he has already moved back into the bad wheat. Snow flowers on his hands.

"This is not a painting," he says. "These are my clothes." In his fields the phone becomes the villain. "Do not look at the eagles," he says.

He cannot tell where one name begins and another falls away. His corridors collapse when the noon rain arrives. I do not look at the eagles.

1: In what city and state do you currently live?

Auburn, AL
San Diego, CA
San Francisco, CA
Santa Monica, CA
Denver, CO x3
West Hartford, CT
Washington, DC
Athens, GA
Atlanta, GA
Iowa City, IA x4
Chicago, IL x2
Edwardsville, IL
Bloomington, IN
Louisville, KY
Northampton, MA
Quincy, MA
Brooklyn, MA
Minneapolis, MN
St. Paul, MN
Lincoln, NE
Bronx, NY
Brooklyn, NY x4
Hastings on Hudson, NY
Rego Park, NY
Portland, OR x2
Providence, RI
Carlisle, PA
Huntsville, TX
Provincial City
Stuttgart, Germany

**JOHN
BEER**
is the author of
*The Waste Land
and Other Poems*
(Canarium,
2010). A former
theater critic
for *Time Out
Chicago,* he
teaches in the
MFA program
at Portland
State University.

THE WASTE LAND

'Aber die Thronen, wo? Die Tempel, und wo die Gefasse,
Wo mit Nectar gefullt, Gottern zu Lust der Gesang?'

'Someone's got it in for me'

for Jack Spicer
the fabber craftsman

I. The Funeral March (Chicago and Orleans)

Once more in the city I cannot name,
the boat city, the city of light,
the city that endures its fall,
the city of pleasures and vicissitudes,
the skier's city, Fun City, the city under the sky,
city of crime and vegetables, Pornograph City,
the city governed by the Lost and Found Department,
cabinet city, city of the bends, the opium city,
Swing City, Archetype City, city of dust,
city that eludes the seven ages, muskrat city,
the island city of daughters and wives,
Sin City, city of sincerity, the cavernous city,
the city of conventions, hat-maker city,
Alphabet City, city of the last and first,
the city called Marrakesh (I know it is not Marrakesh),
industrial city, the city of airplane booze,
center city, the city without shoulders, the city that forgot,
the trampoline city, Abacus City, the city of tears,
the real city (or the city of the desert),
the unreal city (or the city of good will),
the city of rust, of showers, of late-blooming aster,

Hygiene City, the city of logistics—
once more in the city called Halloween
(I know it is not Halloween), I gathered
the five true ingredients of gunpowder
and arranged to meet my younger brother Stetson
next noon at the Heartland Cafe.

Why do you walk with your face turned from me?
All you do is complain and complain.
What is this thing called love? It is nothing
reliable, not like this silk cravat
on which tiny turtles hover
suspended against an amber background.
The knot needs to be loosened. Night has come.
I walk in the garden amid the late-blooming roses
and guard my glass from the moon.
This morning the police came for me.
They brought a letter covered with signs
I could not decipher. They demanded
I register my address properly,
because they are sorely tested by the time's demands
and cannot function as my delivery service.
I met their angry gazes with a sigh, and I proclaimed:
"April is the coolest month, which brings
happy policeman the pleasant dreams of spring."
They still refused to answer my questions.
I know my life is in terrible danger.
What is this thing called love?

II. Don't Look Back

A degree or two to the right
of an imagined meridian

marking time's monotonous ecliptic
tracing and retracing the animal steps
that bring the man down narrow hallways,
a painting hangs, depicting
an almond tree in blossom, unfurling
white petals against a deepening green,
brown brushstrokes scarring the field,
and in the center of the decentered vista,
a fleck of canvas erupts through the paint,
as when air thrusts itself to fill a vacuum,
or after galactic gyrations the light
of a now-cold star reveals itself to us
and breaks the settled pattern of the sky.
For if the tree implies a quiet place
where pendulums might rest,
the heart decline to beat, a place
of time disclosing the lattice of time,
each node identical, complete within itself,
its infinite simplicity sufficient
to lure the mind out of its droning dream
of traffic, footstools, marzipan, and clouds
back to itself, if the tree must be a sign
of the viewer's hunger to escape from signs
and thereby lose the world, the tiny scar
unmakes the fiction that sustains the tree,
the way a cashier's knowing jibe
at the record you had waited weeks to buy,
recommended to you by a woman you barely know
who mentioned it in passing, then returned
to her diatribe against the host who failed
to invite her boyfriend or her companion's boyfriend—
you had only half been listening until she said,
"It sounds like nothing else, not like the wind

or ocean, not even like the early Pixies,
though it has that effect on you, something like
getting a letter addressed to someone else
that ends up addressed to you, in that
reading it with a proper sense of shame
throws your devotion to formalities
completely out the window. I think they're from New York,"
and meant to ask her how the band was spelled,
but the moment had passed, your cigarettes were out,
and the birdless night grew colder. You returned
to people you felt more familiar with,
the oddly Teutonic name in the back of your mind,
and only later came across it in the discount bin
of the Princeton Record Exchange, whose clerks
everyone knows are assholes, so the sneer
on the Tom Verlaine guy's lips was no surprise,
though it gripped you with a sense as far from panic
as it resembled exile. No song can bear
the weight we need to place upon it;
nothing returns as we ask it to return.

O O that T. S. Eliot
he's such a shrinking violet
and if you think I sigh a lot
try life with T. S. Eliot

Sam's problem was he would always compare himself
to other people. I told him, Sam, you don't need to be
a hero. But now I can see I was wrong. I wanted him
to be heroic, but not in that guerilla-theater way.
I told him, Sam, it's time to take off the puppet head.
You could give him a little credit, though, for standing up
against corporate hegemony. He always buys his coffee

from locally owned establishments, and he shoplifts
all those books of poetry from Barnes and Noble.
Oh, everyone deserves a little credit. All the angry
little men in angry little rooms can write
their diagnoses, xerox their zines, and dream
that someday they'll become the next Debord.
In the meantime, how am I supposed to live?
None of us is getting any younger. Power clutches
THANK YOU FOR SHOPPING AT BORDERS.
WE WILL BE CLOSING IN FIFTEEN MINUTES.
everyone with a velvet embrace. But isn't
a life deformed by constant struggle a life
as much defined by power's rule as one
in which you carve a space out for yourself?
I want to find my happiness on my own terms.
That's what we all want—isn't it? At least,
THANK YOU FOR SHOPPING AT BORDERS.
WE WILL BE CLOSING IN FIFTEEN MINUTES.
thank God, we live in a day and age
where people aren't afraid to talk about orgasms.
Speaking of which, you've got to go see
the Orphee that just opened at Performers' Collective.
All the actors have been in car crashes,
and they've added an orgy—it's a little derivative,
but what isn't, these days? OK, got to run,
ciao, I'll see you later, love to all.
THANK YOU FOR SHOPPING AT BORDERS.
WE WILL BE CLOSING IN FIFTEEN MINUTES.

THANK YOU FOR SHOPPING AT BORDERS.
WE WILL BE CLOSING IN FIFTEEN MINUTES.

III. Ballad of the Police Department

"Loving a music man ain't always
what it's supposed to be," she thought
as the fang pierced her heel and she sank.
This is the song of love and the law,
of what is enduring and what disappears.

Dissolving, her eye met its twin in the water
(or was it a glass in the guise of a stream?)
In the cafe, the boys drank to Orpheus.
Encircled by drafts on the tables and floor,
he waved a half-wave and lit a Gitane.

Sirens we were used to, but so early?
Through a window specked by last night's rain,
I saw Wojohowicz give him the news,
then returned to my book: *The Invention of Chance*.
This is the song of atomic decay.

Contemporary fascination
with corporal preservation
recapitulates the ancient
ceremonies of atonement,
or so, at least, it seems to me,
as I lecture empty rooms
on F. H. Bradley and the moon.
Not the moon you lovers see,
the moon as it appears to me
and me alone, my eyes refined
by distillation in the mind.
My moon rains light through long night hours
awake within the prison tower

of internal experience,
the tower holding thief and prince,
stockbroker and the child of fame,
identically, but not the same.
One hears the scraping of the key.
One wishes one were one, not me.

Through darkness he descended to the platform.
One quarter struck another. Buskers
danced in supplication of the shadows,
mirroring the disgraced King of Pop.
White noise announced the train. Orpheus wept.

After North and Clybourn comes Division,
and after Division, the final law, whose lord
sits anxiously beside his stolen bride.
I will not pretend I know the song he sang
before the dreadful pair. You know the stories

as well as I: that from the gramaphone
a swell of scratch and hurl and gem-like glint,
of vouchsafed soul and breakbeats reconciled,
shattered the shale resolve of Death himself:
edict turned to grace. But I can still

remind you of the lesson coming up,
paused as we are at the axis of our hope.
Necessity may, for a moment, yield to love,
but love explodes each moment in its drive
to the next, and the next, and the next, like footsteps—

With a sudden cry Sgt. Wojo averred:
"The song of policemen has yet to be heard!

You can call it ignoble, or even absurd,
But my comrades have hung on each sibilant word,
And we've waited and waited as locations blurred
From subway to Hades: we've yet to be heard!"
Amid shouts of sha-hoobla, tik-tak, and tra-lay,
The song of policemen now carried the day.
Brass buttons new polished, bright jackets fresh-pressed,
And riot protectors protecting their chests,
From buses and wagons policemen erupted,
From storefronts and stations, and, uninterrupted,
They sang as they rounded up each interloper:
Each anti-war chanter, each car window soaper.
They sang like a city-sized 8-track recorder,
And phalanxed, Miranda'ed, preserved the disorder
That the bravest policeman felt clutch at his heart
From the untamed community begging his art.
"Hey-hey-o," they sang, and such pleasant palaver
And then morning came. They were walking cadavers.
They might tell funny stories, or wrestle, or shout,
But something—divine spark? the soul?—had gone out.
And all of the people and all of the streets
And all of the sweet shops where young lovers meet
Invisibly withered, and no one could say
Where the deadness had come from, how long it might stay.
But now Wojohowicz regrets his decision
To insert himself. There will be no revision.
So he takes off his hat and he gives up his gun
And that's how the song of policemen is done.

Where were you then?
I was at North and Clybourn.

No one was with you?

I was alone.

And Death's dispensation?
       It came with conditions.

Conditions you flouted?
       I slipped. The underworld does not forgive.

When all aloud the wind is blowing,
  And coughing drowns the poet's song,
And terminals brood softly glowing,
  And Marian wears a blue sarong,

When synthecrabs squirm in the beaker,
Then nightly hums the opaque speaker
      Tu-who;
Tu-whit, tu-who—a subtle note,
While Joan stirs on in a distant plot.

Arm. The words of Mercury are oddly muted after the studies of Jessie Weston.
You, that way: we, this way.

IV. Gaza Strip

          A current under sea
Picked his bones in whispers. And this I know.
Forgot the way of gulls. He rose and fell.
His teeth as white as snow.

A current under sea. O you
Walk her every day into the deep sea swell.

She passed the stages of her age and youth.
Orpheus wept. I think it's love.

O you who turn the wheel,
Consider how his bones were picked,
A fortnight dead. And this I know.
Gentile or Phoenician, dark Don Juan,
I think it's love. I think it's love. As tall as you.

V. Death to Poetry

Orpheus awoke in the poem of disguises, the poem once called "The Waste Land."
Friends, listen up. He gathered the remnants of the life he had dreamed. He
renounced the burden of the name he bore. He began to walk.

Orpheus walked down Milwaukee Avenue toward the Flatiron Building. He
passed bodegas, taquerias, vintage stores. He met a hustler with a gas can. He
walked past the anarchist kids. And he walked, and he walked, and he walked
past the cabdrivers trading insults in Urdu, and he walked past convenience
stores, and he walked past Latin Kings, and he walked past waitresses getting
off night shifts, and he walked past jazz stars that nobody recognized, he walked
past the students, the teachers, the cops. And the sky was the color of eggplant
and tire fires, the sky was the field that resisted exhaustion. And he walked, and
he walked past the puddles and gutters. And no one walked with him. And SUVs
burned, and the asphalt ran liquid and Orpheus saw the dissolving sky and he
knew that the name of the poem he had entered could not be "The Waste Land" or
even "White Phosphorus," or "The Song of Policemen." In his pocket he fingered
a tiny slip of paper. He opened and read it. It said, "This is the death of the poet."
And yes. And yes. This is the death of the poet.

Shhhh. I am allergic to melodrama.

Shhhh. The serpent encircles the world.

Shhhh. There is a plausible explanation.

But watch it! the daughters of Ismara,
Their heaving chests wrapped up in beastly fleece,
From their hilltop perch, catch sight of Orpheus
Smithing his voice to match plucked strings.
Cunctaque tela forent cantu mollita, sed ingens
Clamor et infracto Berecyntia tibia cornu
Typanaque et plausus et Bacchei ululatus
Obstrepuere sono citharae, tum denique saxa
Non exauditi rubuerunt sanguine vatis.
And the stones grew red with the blood of the poet.
These footnotes have I shored against my ruins.
These footnotes
                    shhhh
                                      we set foot
in a world ash-sick, a bad dream world
no longer the mirror, no longer the poem

the birdless night grew colder

And once the poem ended, commentary began. I said, I, the author, said, "Or-
pheus is a mask in a poem infected with masks." I said, "The importance of
footnotes cannot be overestimated." I said, "The essential problem of the poem is
the essential problem of our time, of all time: how to love one another." And I was
not, readers, Orpheus, and I did not descend into the depths, and I have only these
words to defend me, and the shadows, the shadows howl for my blood

Once more in the city he refused to name
a phenomenon that I have often noticed

Once more in the city that endures its fall
Well then I'll fix you. Mackie's back in town
Once more in the city called Barnes and Noble
an elaborate deception, like a bird
Once more in the city that everyone forgot
and swerved to catch the sun on its wing
cf. McGinty, Possum Among the Hoopoes
a broken face, a city of dust and telescopy
abandoned the ruse that had once been the poem
and listened as the buildings lightly sang:

Oh we'll meet again
When all the rained out faces
And all the bomb-scarred places
Kiss me kiss me kiss me
Under the telegraphic moon
And I won't get up, I won't
Get up, I'll never, never, never

2: What is your shoe size?

female:

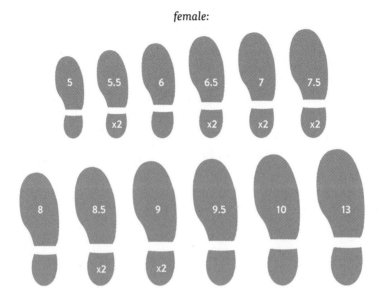

male:

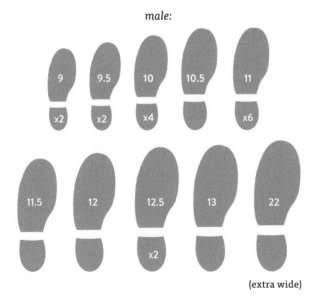

(extra wide)

NICKY
BEER
is the author of
*The Diminishing
House* (Carnegie
Mellon, 2010). She
has been awarded a
literature fellowship
from the National
Endowment for the
Arts, a Ruth Lilly
Fellowship from the
Poetry Foundation,
a scholarship and
fellowship from
the Bread Loaf
Writers' Conference,
a "Discovery"/*The
Nation* award, and
a Campbell Corner
Prize. She is an
assistant professor
at the University of
Colorado Denver.

AVUNCULARITY

Every child ought to have a dead uncle.
There should be only one surviving photograph,
or else a handful of epochal snapshots
where the face is always blurred, in half-light,
or otherwise indistinct. Much can made of
the raised glass in his hand and the quirked
corners of his smile. And who was that girl
standing with him? Ellie? Jean? No, the one
from Pittsburgh with the dogs.
You hadn't been born then anyway . . .
This is the one whose fault it can be:
the slight warps, the spider-cracks in your speech,
the explanation for all of the wrongness
that made the other children pause, assess you
a little coldly and pull back as one toward the playground.
Why all of the strange words seem to rise
from your tongue like damp, nocturnal creatures
into an unwelcoming light. Why you insist
on that turd-brown jacket that smells like
a musty fruitcake. Why that one thumbnail
is always gnawed to a puffed red crescent.
This man will be your phantom limb,
the thing once flesh, thrust into absence,
now living as a restless pricking under your skin,
that inward itching, that impossible,
inescapable rue fretting to itself,
the way the mouth tries to form urgent words
in a dream. And you'll take out that picture
so that your eyes can retrace the details:
red shirt, a vague mess of books
and cards on the table, half of one silver

aluminum can, a bright nova hovering
over his left shoulder as though something
has chosen that moment to rush into his body.
See, see there, his buttons are done
wrong. He must have forgotten things
all the time, just like you.

PROVENANCE

One of the workmen will be pulling down
the old paneling, enjoying how easily
it comes away from the wall, the nails sliding
from their holes with a rusty *frisson*.
About a yard of plaster will lay bare before
he uncovers what he'll think is wallpaper,
the pattern a faded landscape in miniature,
or the silhouettes of lean clouds over a dune,
or schools of brown eels. But then
he will recognize the word "unyielding," then "thighbone":
your copperplate, some seventy years out of fashion,
slanting across the west and north walls from ceiling
to wainscoting—one hundred poems pasted under the wood,
untitled, separated with microscopic Roman numerals.
It will be a genteel kind of shock, like finding a ghost
who does not know he is a ghost, content to amble
in circles around the same garret, murmuring
mild-mannered exclamations in threadbare shirtsleeves.
You'd done this so that when they came
to take your typewriter, it could go
with them silent and blameless to render
its dutiful cha-cha for a neophyte clerk
with a quiet passion for the stenographer's knees.
It would not be able to say how the city became
a nightmare of starlings, the evening air a plague
of tinny fugues. Or how love was like an orange,
a thing to be stripped with one's fingernails,
split by the seams of its bitter pith and made to weep
a sweetness which burns in the cracked corners
of an open mouth. A ceiling leak had cut a bleeding
trail through your ode to _____, something

all at once *angel and machine, rocking us into dreams*
while the earth splits against history's sullen plow.
You'd named yourself a joiner, a rag-picker,
knitting together a day's scurf into poetry. *One can only be*
sure of the pieces—the whole is the business of God alone.
All our art is dumb luck anyway, a morbid nursery rhyme
of diminishment: for every one of our masterpieces,
there's one rotting to threads behind a screen
in the asylum, one crushed to mortar in the siege,
one blamelessly lost in a street bazaar,
one binding the wound of the heretic,
one in a house burned to its stone roots before the renovations,
consigning us to only the signature of flame.

AD HOMINEM

The Poet:
Fugitive lung, prodigal intestine—
where's the pink crimp in my side
where they took you out?

The Octopus:
It must be a dull world, indeed,
where everything appears
to be a version or extrapolation
of you.

The birds are you.
The springtime is you.
Snails, hurricanes, saddles, elevators—
everything becomes
you.

I, with a shift
of my skin, divest my self
to become the rock
that shadows it.

Think of when
your reading eyes momentarily drift,
and in that instant

you see the maddening swarm of alien ciphers submerged within the text

gone before you can focus.
That's me.

Or your dozing revelation
on the subway that you are
slowly being
digested. Me again.

I am the fever dream
in which you see your loved ones
as executioners. I am also their axe.

Friend, while you're exhausting
the end of a day
with your sad approximations,

I'm a mile deep
in the earth, vamping
my most flawless impression
of the abyss

to the wild applause of eels.

BLACK HOLE ITINERARY

Today they will offer me a dozen mirrors
and tell me to pick the one with my real face in it.

Today she'll be swimming out into the ocean to find me
and today I'll be the wave that drowns her.

Today they'll say *God has a plan for all of us*
and she'll say *God is a Cruel Motherfucker today.*

Today I'll be the bird in my head
getting fat on the sweet grey taffy of old time.

Today I will be immortal
but they'll keep setting me on fire just to check.

Today she'll summon beasts of protection
by strumming the scars on my back.

Today the spider will keep me alive for a week
before dining off of my eyes.

Today my total gravity will be monstrous.

Today they'll make me repeat her name
until its atoms split apart.

Today love will be like starlight:
when it arrives, whatever it comes from will have already collapsed.

**CIARAN
BERRY**

is a 2012 Whiting Award winner. Originally from the West of Ireland, he has lived in the United States for the past fifteen years. His first book, *The Sphere of Birds,* won the Crab Orchard Series in Poetry Open Competition and was published by Southern Illinois University Press. The same book was published by The Gallery Press in Ireland and the UK, where it won the Jerwood Aldeburgh First Collection Prize and the inaugural Michael Murphy Memorial Prize. Recent work has appeared in *AGNI, Crazyhorse, Ploughshares,* and *The Threepenny Review.* He's currently working on a second manuscript titled *The Dead Zoo.*

THE PARSLEY NECKLACE

Before he gives himself up to the air that swirls and eddies
        there just after dawn, Petit tests the steel wire with his toes,
            makes that tensioned cable his own, a sort of extra limb
that will hold him more than a thousand feet above Church Street,

        where the rush hour crowd, jackets over their arms, spill
            from the subway scuffle. They are no bigger than a swarm of flies
from where the wire walker hangs his eye, feels for the fulcrum
        in his balancing pole, and then, with a sharp intake of breath,

            takes his first step, trusts where he must go. All of this happens
thirty years ago, when I'm just four, a nervous middle child
        who takes sick on every car journey of more than five miles,
            retches and heaves until there's nothing left but yellow bile.

My mother's tried a series of folk-cures—a length of chain
        suspended from the rusted tow bar to spark all the static
            out of the car, a parsley necklace fixed around my throat,
where it serves as a sort of vegetable amulet, but nothing works.

        Something about the body's wish to move at its own pace,
            resistance to the confined space of our beige Renault 4,
another fear to add to a list that includes German shepherds,
        earwigs, heights. I never leave the house without a pocketful

            of plastic bags. On his high wire, Petit moves with the grace
of a gymnast, his walk is pure dream work, a sort of being
        and, at the same time, not being within the confines of his
            skinny frame, this conclusion to what began with a toothache,

in a Paris dentist's waiting room: on a table there the magazine
        in which he found a sketch of the new towers and traced a line
                between those roofs to make the distance smaller, more bridgeable.
Spreading the photos now over my desk, I wonder what Hart Crane

        would make of this, the Brooklyn Bridge suspended somewhere
                over Petit's shoulder as he steps towards the center of the wire
and genuflects to acknowledge the crowd he knows will have
        gathered below with their briefcases and half-smoked cigarettes,

                each head tilted back, each mouth and pair of eyes opened into
the same stunned look of those who sat on deck the morning
        Crane appeared, still drunk and unshaven, one eye blackened
                from his brawl with the cabin boy he wanted only to love,

mournful as he draped his coat over the railings and, wearing
        just his pajamas, plunged into the gulf, where his body became
                so much sand and foam. In this moment, where everything
is pure present, and these black & whites are something I can

        almost step into, it is Crane's shade that hovers a few feet
                above Petit in the shape of the all-seeing gull that catches
the tightrope walker's eye as he lays out on the wire, defying
        all the bones in his body, right leg crooked for balance, left leg

                dangling free, only those few inches between him and an almighty fall.
Or else the gull is death personified, arrived to stare our hero
        out, hoping soon to knock him off kilter and bear him away
                into the whatever. Although Petit only stares back and smiles,

then rises, steps towards the other side, where a young cop waits,

amazed, with one hand on his gun. On long journeys, smoke
        of my father's pipe billowing, the parsley necklace dying
round my throat, I'd stare out the window and count telephone

    poles, trying to make the journey go quicker, trying to trick
        my body towards false calm. I'd keep a total in increments
of ten, lose my place and start over. It was another way
    for me to learn about the beginning, the end, the in between.

AT NERO'S CIRCUS

Dressed up as dogs, they're torn apart by dogs,
           nailed to their own crosses, or set aflame
      as if to prove the body's wax around
the soul's frail wick. If the scribe's to be
         believed, a martyr chooses death. Therefore,
      our emperor gives them what they desire.
Through a spyglass of cut emerald, he stares
         down at the spectacle,

the lake of blood the Christians bathe in tinged
         with green. He loves to play the lute and has
      a knack for allegory. He burned our city
just to sing of Troy. "Oh nest of our fathers,
         oh dear cradle," he intoned, plucking one
      gold string. To please the flesh, he'd do
just about anything—sleep with his mother,
         put her to the sword.

With the blood gorging the loins swollen, it
         begins; with the eyes scratched by daylight
      in their first stunned seconds beyond the womb—
the pang and grapple that drives the animal
         to this, his circus, which abuts the cemetery,
      where, between killings, the mythic beasts
are led in one by one. The tiger's swagger.
         The four-legged mountain

of the elephant. We applaud. We take it in.
         The pupil fills its empty bowl again,
      again. Is there nothing it would not eat?
Here is where we stuck their Peter upside

down, and here, too, where they'll lay foundations
for his church. Our spear-shaped obelisk
they'll place at the center of the square, symbol,
they'll say, of how we reach

up to their Christ. If only we could read
better our symbols—the hounds biting at heels
until they've felled both bull and believer,
the horses, all sweat and blinker, leading out
our famed charioteers. They are the same horses
the emperor will hear later when, betrayed
by his pleasures, he takes up a knife
to slit his own fine throat.

AT BALLYCONNEELY

On 2 August 1908 a mirage of a faraway city was seen at Ballyconneely, on the Connemara coast. It was described as a city of different-sized houses, in different styles of architecture, and was visible for over three hours.
—Foster's Irish Oddities

Who knows, if you look long enough,
what might blossom up out of the spume?
Dead man's fingers, gutweed, Neptune's necklace,
plastic bottles from Vladivostok and Gdansk,

or an entire town, floodlit at midnight
and, it appeared, floating out there beyond
the range of cormorants, the black
and whiskered buoys that turned out to be seals,

while the whole village gathered at the pier
puffing on clay pipes, consoling grandchildren,
until someone said it must be New York
and someone else Boston, from where

her stunned sister had just sent a letter home
folded three times over a lone dollar
and describing the taste of a Bartlett pear,
the man from Clare she'd met at a church dance.

The ginger Conroy twins stood holding hands
as if their drowned father's return
was imminent, as if his upturned currach
had just beached somewhere out there,

and not gone down broken among whale
graveyards, wrasse and mackerel shoals.
While the widow Lynch dropped to her knees,
fingered her beads, and swore the savior

would walk soon again upon the water,
come ashore here to black tea, brown bread,
sean nós singers, to a landscape stone-
pocked and strange as the red face of Mars,

or the dirt floor of that half-made heaven
in Signorelli's painting where, legged
and armed again, naked and toned,
the dead welcome one another into an afterlife

that appears much the same as the before.
No one said mirage. No one said a reflection of the moon.
No one said Shangri La. No one said Xanadu.
That's not the sort of people that they were.

And because the gnarled, barnacled rocks lurk
just below that broken stretch of coast,
no one dared take a boat out there before dawn.
For the meantime, for their own separate reasons,

those Maddens, Mealys, Gorhams, and McLanes
waited for something, not quite sure
whether they were waiting for the seraphim
to fill their dimpled cheeks and blow their horns,

the groan of thole pins and the splash of oars
that might welcome some hero out of folklore home,
or the propeller drone as a biplane bearing
Alcock & Brown came down out of cloud,

swooped shrike-like towards heather and gorse,
the whiskey that kept them warm still wet
on their breaths, and on their tongues,
news of the new world, salt from Atlantic foam.

3: Do you speak another language?

Badly,
Rarely,
Sometimes,
A Little,
Not Well,
I Try

Yes	I Try	No
17	13	10

English
French x7
Hebrew
Irish
Japanese
Portuguese
Russian
Spanish x5

**JERICHO
BROWN**
is an assistant professor
at Emory University. His
poems have appeared
or are forthcoming
in journals and
anthologies including
*American Poetry Review,
Boston Review, The New
Yorker, Oxford American,
The New Republic,* and
Best American Poetry. His
first book, *Please* (New
Issues, 2008), won the
American Book Award,
and his second book,
The New Testament,
is forthcoming from
Copper Canyon Press.

TRACK 1: LUSH LIFE

The woman with the microphone sings to hurt you,
To see you shake your head. The mic may as well
Be a leather belt. You drive to the center of town
To be whipped by a woman's voice. You can't tell
The difference between a leather belt and a lover's
Tongue. A lover's tongue might call you *bitch,*
A term of endearment where you come from, a kind
Of compliment preceded by the word *sing*
In certain nightclubs. A lush little tongue
You have: you can yell, *Sing bitch,* and, *I love you,*
With a shot of Patrón at the end of each phrase
From the same barstool every Saturday night, but you can't
Remember your father's leather belt without shaking
Your head. That's what satisfies her, the woman
With the microphone. She does not mean to entertain
You, and neither do I. Speak to me in a lover's tongue—
Call me your bitch, and I'll sing the whole night long.

TRACK 5: SUMMERTIME

as performed by Janis Joplin

God's got his eye on me, but I ain't a sparrow.
I'm more like a lawn mower . . . no, a chainsaw,
Anything that might mangle each manicured lawn
In Port Arthur, a place I wouldn't return to
If the mayor offered me every ounce of oil
My daddy cans at the refinery. My voice, I mean,
Ain't sweet. Nothing nice about it. It won't fly
Even with Jesus watching. I don't believe in Jesus.
The Baxter boys climbed a tree just to throw
Persimmons at me. The good and perfect gifts
From above hit like lightning, leave bruises.
So I lied—I believe, but I don't think God
Likes me. The girls in the locker room slapped
Dirty pads across my face. They called me
Bitch, but I never bit back. I ain't a dog.
Chainsaw, I say. My voice hacks at you. I bet
I tear my throat. I try so hard to sound jagged.
I get high and say one thing so many times
Like Willie Baker who worked across the street—
I saw some kids whip him with a belt while he
Repeated, *Please*. School out, summertime
And the living lashed, Mama said I should be
Thankful, that the town's worse to coloreds
Than they are to me, that I'd grow out of my acne.
God must love Willie Baker—all that leather and still
A please that sounds like music. See.
I wouldn't know a sparrow from a mockingbird.
The band plays. I just belt out, *Please*. This tune
Ain't half the blues. I should be thankful.
I get high and moan like a lawn mower
So nobody notices I'm such an ugly girl.

I'm such an ugly girl. I try to sing like a man
Boys call, *boy*. I turn my face to God. I pray. I wish
I could pour oil on everything green in Port Arthur.

TIN MAN

In my chest

Drop a penny.

Cities shine gray.

No green is god.

And every tree must fall,

A missing beat.

Man made me.

Pull the lever:

So I stop.

Your whole world

The color gray.

Can I get you

Tired of your body?

Beat time—

a slit of air.

I can't feel a thing.

Never believe

I've watched color die.

slicing the air.

Skip it—

Add a little oil,

I chop.

I am tired

unpaved, green.

Don't you want

an axe handle

Use mine.

I won't feel

Don't say love.

Remember

the color green.

I've killed it.

In my chest

Hush, love.

drop one penny,

Men made me

of your woods,

Cities shine

something heartless?

for destruction?

Manhandle,

one damn thing.

4: What's your favorite reading series?

Any that take place in a bar
Bad Shadow Affair, Denver, CO x2
Bridge Street, Washington, DC
Chin Music Series, Brooklyn, NY x2
College of Staten Island Series
Danny's Reading Series, Chicago, IL x6
First Person Plural, Harlem, NY
Happy Ending (Amanda Stern's series), New York, NY
In Your Ear, Washington, DC
KGB Bar Reading Series, New York, NY x2
Monsters of Poetry, Madison, WI x3
O. B. Hardison Poetry Series, Washington, DC
Observable Readings, St. Louis, MO
One Pause Poetry, Ann Arbor, MI
Pitt Contemporary Writers, Pittsburgh, PA
Poetry and Biscuits, Chicago, IL
Poetry Project, New York, NY
Poetry Time at Space Space (defunct), New York, NY
Publicity Complex, Providence, RI
Segue, New York, NY
Studio One Reading Series, Oakland, CA
The New Privacy, Portland, Oregon
The *Rain Taxi* Reading Series
The River Styx at the Tavern (formerly Duff's) Series, St. Louis, MO
Vox, Athens, GA

SUZANNE BUFFAM

is the author of
two collections
of poetry: *Past
Imperfect* (House
of Anansi) and
The Irrationalist
(Canarium),
which was a
finalist for the
2011 Griffin Prize.
Born and raised
in Canada, she
lives in Chicago.

THE NEW EXPERIENCE

I was ready for a new experience.
All the old ones had burned out.

They lay in little ashy heaps along the roadside
And blew in drifts across the fairgrounds and fields.

From a distance some appeared to be smoldering
But when I approached with my hat in my hands

They let out small puffs of smoke and expired.
Through the windows of houses I saw lives lit up

With the otherworldly glow of TV
And these were smoking a little bit too.

I flew to Rome. I flew to Greece.
I sat on a rock in the shade of the Acropolis

And conjured dusky columns in the clouds.
I watched waves lap the crumbling coast.

I heard wind strip the woods.
I saw the last living snow leopard

Pacing in the dirt. Experience taught me
That nothing worth doing is worth doing

For the sake of experience alone.
I bit into an apple that tasted sweetly of time.

The sun came out. It was the old sun,
With only a few billion years left to shine.

ENOUGH

I am wearing dark glasses inside the house
To match my dark mood.

I have left all the sugar out of the pie.
My rage is a kind of domestic rage.

I learned it from my mother
Who learned it from her mother before her

And so on.
Surely the Greeks had a word for this.

Now, surely the Germans do.
The more words a person knows

To describe her private sufferings,
The more distantly she can perceive them.

I repeat the names of all the cities I've known
And watch an ant drag its crooked shadow home.

What does it mean to love the life we've been given?
To act well the part that's been cast for us?

Wind. Light. Fire. Time.
A train whistles through the far hills.

One day I plan to be riding it.

MARINER

Sometimes I eat an orange and completely forget about dying. Nonetheless, the thought of home can reliably be said to bring tears to the eyes of any traveller. When the sailor travels inland, he misses not so much the sight of the ocean as the sound it makes beneath him at night when the world has disappeared and there are only stars above to guide him. Perhaps he also misses the smell of creosote in the breeze, but it remains so utterly abstract in its absence he cannot properly be said to *feel* the lack. On the other hand, I find it possible to miss what I have never known. My voice has been described as nondescript, yet I continue to use it. I call to the hills and to the good people in them. I call to hear the sound of my own voice. The truth is, I seldom think about home at all. To grow up at sea is a mixed blessing, granted, but show me a blessing that isn't.

A PERFECT EMERGENCY

It was already aflame when I spotted it there in the parking lot.

Kids were standing around throwing sticks at it, kicking dirt in its
        face.

All I could do was look on in pity as it thrashed at the air like a
        tiny, vengeful sun.

But like a tiny, vengeful sun, the burning bush didn't want pity.
        When I approached with my hands in my pockets, it shook out
        its golden locks and sang in a language I could see.

I am the Unburnt Bush! it cried. *I am Burning but Flourishing! I am*
        Swallowed but I am not Consumed!

In my head was a page from a musty old book with its useless list
        of Latin verbs. Before me I could see all the lives I might have
        lived, lined up and leaping through the same burning gate.

It was a perfect emergency. The only thing worth saving was the
        blaze.

5: In what city and state were you born?

Casa Grande, AZ
Berkeley, CA
Upland, CA
Colorado Springs, CO
Greeley, CO
New Haven, CT
Washington, DC x2
Fort Wayne, IN
Topeka, KS
Wichita, KS x2
Shreveport, LA
New Bedford, MA
Newton, MA
Baltimore, MD
Lansing, MI
Motor City, MI
St. Louis, MO
Minneapolis, MN
Wolfeboro, NH

Newark, NJ
Metuchen, NJ
Albany, NY
Huntington, NY
Staten Island, NY
Dayton, OH
Euclid, OH
Providence, RI
Warwick, RI
Galveston, TX
Provo, UT
McLean, VA
Pullman, WA
Afro-Future, Freedom State
Nuremberg, Germany
Dublin, Ireland
Guadalajara, Mexico
Yokohama, Japan
Montreal, Quebec

HEATHER CHRISTLE is the author of *The Difficult Farm* (Octopus, 2009), *The Trees The Trees* (Octopus, 2011), and *What Is Amazing* (Wesleyan, 2012). She has recently taught at Antioch College and Sarah Lawrence College, and is the web editor of *jubilat*.

IT'S NOT A GOOD SHORTCUT IF EVERYONE DIES

Yesterday, looking at a cinderblock's
reflection—lightest grey on golden floor—
I finally understood painting. I was irate!
I took a sledgehammer to the cinderblock,
but as it was supporting the terrarium,
I smashed that as well, and the floor was badly
damaged and the walls weakened, and running
outside to see my house collapse, I finally
understood architecture. I was irate! I went
door to door, to my neighbors, trying to explain
the system we actually inhabit, and they became
absorbed, so we all flapped our arms together
and though we did not fly away I finally
understood how geese make decisions. I was
crushed. I wandered the earth for eighteen years,
honking at anyone who'd listen and there were
a few who even fell in love with me, but because
they did not understand I was under a powerful
spell they could not help me, so I walked sadly
north, migrating so slowly I never reached
anywhere, and in my deceleration I finally
understood infinity's paradox and I myself began
to shrink until my head was too small to contain
much of anything—I'm down to quarks, an idea
so tiny it's sometimes not even there and it suits
me—I appear, the thought appears: quark.

ACORN DULY CRUSHED

Dear stupid forest.
Dear totally brain-dead forest.
Dear beautiful ugly stupid forest
full of nightingales
why won't you shut up.
What do you want from me.
A train is too expensive.
A clerk will fall asleep.
Dear bitchy stupendous forest.
Trade seats with me.
Now it is your birthday.
Congrats!
Someone will probably slap you
about the face and ears.
Indulgent municipal forest.
Forest of scarves and of beards.
Dear rapid bloodless forest
you are talking all the time.
You are not pithy.
You are like 8,000 swans.
Dear nasty pregnant forest.
You are so hot!
You are environmentally significant.
Men love to hang themselves
from your standard old growth trees.
Don't look at me.
You are the one with
the ancient noble terror.
Bad forest. Forest with
important gangs of leaves.

Dear naïve forest,
what won't you be admitting!
Blunt international forest.
Forest of bees and of hair.
You should come back to my house.
We can bag drugs all night.
You can tell me
about your new windows.
How they are just now
beginning to sprout.

THAT AIR OF RUTHLESSNESS IN SPRING

here is the hand   here is the hand   on my
face   it's not my hand   it's a beautiful
day   again   I can hardly believe anything
what   about   you   who   are   so   frequently
touching   some part of the world   what is
it you're touching today   when I touch the
trees   the trees think *man-child*   they are
so wrong   but it is a human face I put on
I am hung up under this weather   I am
hanging on tight   to a swing   when I go
up enough I jump   then I am not touching
anything   then the world thinks I've
disappeared   I am just having a little fun
not much fun at all   are you sad   did you
touch the world   the wrong way
everything is always happening   and not
just for show   I want to show you
something   I don't care what   I want you
to look where I say

BASIC

This program is designed to move a white line
from one side of the screen to the other.

This program is not too hard, but it has
a sad ending and that makes people cry.

This program is designed to make people cry
and step away when they are finished.

In one variation the line moves diagonally
up and in another diagonally down.

This makes people cry differently,
diagonally. A whole room of people

crying in response to this program's
variations results in beautiful music.

This program is designed to make such
beautiful music that it feels like at last

they have allowed you to take the good canoe
into a lake of your own choosing

and above you the sky exposes one
or two real eagles, the water

warm or marked with stones,
however you like it, blue.

**EDUARDO C.
CORRAL**
is a CantoMundo
fellow. His poems
have appeared or
are forthcoming in
Beloit Poetry Journal,
jubilat, New England
Review, Ploughshares,
and *Poetry.* His work
has been honored
with a "Discovery"/
The Nation award
and residencies
from the MacDowell
Colony and Yaddo.
He has served as the
Olive B. O'Connor
Fellow in Creative
Writing at Colgate
University and as the
Philip Roth Resident
in Creative Writing
at Bucknell Universi-
ty. *Slow Lightning,* his
first book of poems,
was selected by Carl
Phillips as the 2011
winner of the Yale
Series of Younger
Poets competition.

OUR COMPLETION: OIL ON WOOD: TINO RODRÍGUEZ: 1999

Before nourishment there must be obedience.
In his hands I was a cup overflowing with thirst.
Eighth ruler of my days, ninth lord of my nights:
he thrashed above me, like branches. Once,
after weeks of rain, he sliced a potato in half
to remind me of the moon. The dark slept in the small
of his back. The back of his knees: pale music.
We'd crumble the Eucharist & feed it to the pigeons.
Sin vergüenza. Escuintle. He Who Makes Things Sprout.
In the margins in a book of poems by Emily Dickinson
he scribbled: *she had a pocketful of horses/ Trojan/*
& some of them used. Often I mistook him for a storyteller
when he stood in the rain. A su izquierda, huesos.
A su derecha, mapas de cuero. When I'd yawn,
he'd pluck black petals out of my mouth.

ACQUIRED IMMUNE DEFICIENCY SYNDROME

At a quarter to midnight,
blue beetles crawling
along the minute hand
of the wall clock,
I awaken, panicked,
next to my lover,

a caramel-hued cello asleep
on embroidered linen.
A light bulb blazes,
burns out,
a doe's flash of white tail
that instructs

the fawn to follow its mother
in flight. I hurry down
a hallway, through a door,
into a pasture
where mules are grazing.
Moonlight

floats in the air like coarse cloth,
silver-speckled
& woven on the looms
of mirrors. Once
I tore into the torso of my cello
& discovered

      its heart: a pair of horse shoes
caked with red clay.
                The mules surround me:
necks bent,
      nostrils pluming out different lengths
          of breath.

      I toss off my robe. A mule
curls its tongue around
             my erection. I throw
my head back,
      & stare at the slowest lightning,
          the stars.

TO THE ANGELBEAST

for Arthur Russell

All that glitters isn't music.

Once, hidden in tall grass,
I tossed fistfuls of dirt into the air:
doe after doe of leaping.

You said it was nothing
but a trick of the light. Gold
curves. Gold scarves.

Am I not your animal?

You'd wait in the orchard for hours
to watch a deer
break from the shadows.

You said it was like lifting a cello
out of its black case.

TO A JORNALERO CLEANING OUT MY NEIGHBOR'S GARAGE

for John Olivares Espinoza

You are nothing like my father.

                    And like my father

you are nothing.

             Zambo. Castizo.

Without draft animals

         the Mexica used the wheel

                    only as a toy.

Please keep off the lawn.

             Green mirrors are asleep

beneath the grass.

        In graduate school a landlord asked,

Here to pick strawberries?

         "Y me vine de Hermosillo/

en busca de oro y riqueza."

                  Are your hands

always so dirty?

         Slip a finger in my mouth.

I'll devour the grime

       under the nail.

          Pomegranate, grenade.

Sometimes in order to say a word

             it's necessary

to spit it out. A *spic sells seashells*

        on the seashore. Corrido singers

often consider assonance

        a blemish.

You walk out with a French horn in your arms

             and you're a butcher

in El Dorado holding

     the golden entrails of cattle.

**KYLE
DARGAN**

is the author of three
collections of poetry,
Logorrhea Dementia
(2010), *Bouquet of
Hungers* (2007), and *The
Listening* (2004). For his
work, he has received
the Cave Canem Poetry
Prize, the Hurston/
Wright Legacy Award,
and grants from the D.C.
Commission on the Arts
and Humanities.
Dargan has partnered
with the President's
Committee on the Arts
and Humanities to
produce poetry pro-
gramming at the White
House and Library of
Congress. He is
currently an assistant
professor of literature
and creative writing at
American University
and the founder and
editor of *POST NO ILLS*
magazine.

MELODY FORENSIC

If somebody told me I had only one hour to live,
I'd spend it choking a white man. I'd do it nice and slow.
—Miles Davis

Years in the gristle of knuckles. Thick muscle
at the palm's base. Fingers squeezing,
digging valve keys to mold exhales. Some pain
pinched by the mouthpiece—would it wail
if you had found a pink neck before lead-pipe brass?
Forgive the epigraph. Don't apologize—
your music may taste funny to someone
after reading this. But damn Miles (if I can call you
Miles), why do black men have to scream in art?
What wants off our tongue floats
in the same ether lungs feed metal
(now you got me doing it). Listen,
if "I hurt" falls deaf on their ears,
Kind of Blue is no different.
The black sound congeals in mason jars
lined across the tops of rickety stoves.
We been frying our story, overseasoned
with silences. Miles (I'm calling
you Miles), you don't want to play. Sweet indulgence—
let's pretend we're back at the Five Spot, this poem
just another stage light, move it.
Put the trumpet down. Where would you start?
Maybe there, Mr. Cool at the bar—head lolling,
eyes wilted from your blow,
a coil of saliva in his throat so
sure he can swallow your blue note whole.

I'LL SEE IT WHEN I BELIEVE IT

Ninety-eight percent of people will
die some time in their lives.
—Ricky Bobby

Statistically, one can
prove airplane commutes
to be safer than train travel.
But the statistician fancies
walking to work, as on foot
he is 3.5 times more likely
to meet the potential mother
of his potential children.
Remembering this, he can only muster
a smile for every fourth woman
with whom he manages to share eyes.
At the bread shop, he forces
a stare through the baker's lenses,
yet he longs to decipher her hands,
to know if their powder is sweet
or chalky, though, statistically speaking,
incorporating food into pro-
creation is a poor idea.
We actually all taste alike
when fricasseed in life's ancient roux,
though, statistically, fewer perish
from hunger than specific thirsts
in this world draped with water.
While all data suggests more sinners
walk among us than in hell,
where no pencils endure
and the dead have never bothered
to return the surveys.

STAR-SPANGLED SUTRA

If the weapon be a mask, sand down the dorsal self
      so the mask clings to nothing but the mask.

    *

If the weapon be holy, keep it oiled with doubt—
      the chamber, the forte, the bow's dark joy.

    *

If the weapon be human, draw ligaments snug
      over hollow joints—motion insulated, pooling
      like venom in limbs.

    *

If the weapon be utterance, fix its warhead
      against a knot of air just atop the throat's plummet.

    *

If the weapon be flame, first douse yourself
      with remorse. Distinguish your enemies. Ignite them.

DARCIE DENNIGAN is the author of *Corinna A-Maying the Apocalypse, Madame X,* and *The Dept. of Ephebic Dreamery*. Her work has received awards from the Poetry Society of America, RI State Arts Council, and "Discovery"/ *The Nation*. She teaches at University of Connecticut and co-directs Frequency Writers.

THE ATOLL

Even the children, and the very little ones at that, did not die just any child's death; they pulled themselves together and died that which they already were, and that which they would have become... This and much more have we... very fortuitously... learned from the Atlanteans... The Atlanteans... it was all so very lucky... We'd been testing fission... fusion... fission... They were downwind... just enough... If the rain falls too lightly it's no good... if too heavily... obviously... Upon the lovely dark-haired Atlanteans the rain fell just right... ... ... *All Atlanteans,* we said over the loudspeaker... *All Atlanteans must exit the island...* They were nodding... bowing... Maybe politeness... maybe vomiting... We escorted them... to a very nice... resort-like... laboratory... *Would you like another martini,* we were heard to say... frequently... It turns out... strontium loves... it just loves bones... and cesium 137 rests in the eyes... and gamma rays go right to the blood... And the miracle was... we were hard-pressed to find a morbid... process... That is... none of the Atlanteans made an untimely... Yes there were lesions... sorecuts... And the usual number of miscarriages... maybe a bit more... but nothing too... But the children...! They were the most... Their skin... it began turning... not the gold of tans but of... gold metal... chemically elemental... positively ductile... And their teeth... their teeth had turned ebony immediately... But the amazing... thing... was the glowing ring around each bald kid head...

Dear Atlanteans we are sorry to inform you... But the Atlanteans were... smiling... They... thanked us... patted our lab jackets... Then they turned away from us... They turned back to the children... in the sand... building castles... and alphabets... and... grand frigates... with sand yes... but also with pieces of... They were building pillars of... bone... they built a frieze... with an image of the sun... it was a sun the size of a heart... a heart the size of the fist of a kid... They were playing in the sand with their own skin and organs... *Dear Atlanteans...* We were genuinely sorry... for the mistake... and for what they had mistook... Yet the Atlanteans... such a gracious people... One Atlantean father... picking up a black tooth... the tooth of a child... He smiled... and said... with such solicitousness... *Are you getting all this...?*

THE HALF-LIFE

... We won't have destroyed anything unless we destroy the ruins too... So when the nuclear holocaust happened yesterday, it was bad of course... very bad... for the world... but we were still... we of Bethany Home Hospice... for us, it was... a tonic... for what was... ailing... As head nurse I went... bed-to-bed... giving the residents the... message... *Nuclear free-for-all... world gone... Bethany Home made of nuclear bunker materials... constructed in the 90s... when such things were... on sale... in short...* We had survived and the residents were really... roused... The news... the adrenaline... their lives... for months... might be extended... Clean drinking water wasn't a problem... we had the IV drips... also tuna, Jell-o... enough rice pudding to fill a therapeutic whirlpool... They got a knitting circle going... tried their old hands at wool radiation suits... they knit like crazy... It was great to see their minds off their bodies... But... If we were what was left... We would need to... repopulate... The early onset female dementias had to immediately start shock treatments... in case their minds could make it... if they became pregnant... There were very few men... there are always very few men... but there were some male cases with sperm potential... of course us staffers were mostly past child-bearing age... but Bettina the night nurse's aid and Renaut the night security guy had been on a few breakfast dates... our acutest hope... They... they were given the freshest cans of tuna... Elvira on the third floor... ninety and no help to... Elvira said we could extract her healthy teeth... for dental work... if ever the new baby needed... Really it was... how it should... all the dying ones feeling as if they were merely... everyone putting in bids to have their deathbed be used for Bettina's labor...

But then Bettina and Renaut had their baby... and it was stillborn and... Every single person who still had arms in Bethany Home took turns holding the...

We will try again...! I said... But Bettina and Renaut had... as we were passing around their... left... to build a house of straw in the radioactive wilderness... It was Helen's turn to hold the... Helen had ALS and I had to help... I was crouching down... the infant half in my arms and half in Helen's... Helen said How beautifully easy to break... I said... firmly... Helen it is already broken... But she... she had meant...

me... Then Filomena...the blind diabetic... rubbed my cheek and said it too... So easy to break... *That*... I said... is reality... That's.... nature... The seasons... I said... firmly... There *are* four of them... It *is* spring... It was spring... by the calendar... at least... I am not... young... autumn... if anything... but yes I've embroidered... on my uniform... peaseblossoms... Please they said... Filomena... was fingering the threads... of my peaseblossoms... Please they said... You could so easily... break... It was... IS... my job to... make my patients comfortable... Very well... I slipped a thermometer from my breast pocket... broke it... sipped its liquid mercury... a second thermometer... third... fourth... Filled a clean bedpan with beads of liquid mercury and ate... bibelot after bibelot... But... I continue to exist among them...

THE YOUNGEST LIVING THING IN L.A.

The youngest living thing in L.A. was my baby.
The oldest living thing was the wind.

The wind grew well in that city in the desert.
As did my garden of well-tended cement.
As did my baby, whom I held like a heavy statuette.

I named him *Mill* at his birth... *As the wheel goeth by drift of water...*

And he grew and the wind blew and we lived in that desert and... no rain. No rain, no river. No sound of water. But for—

The fountain water. The official fountain. Which flowed. Every day. Every day the baby slept. The baby breathed. The fountain flowed. It flowed imperceptibly. As if its water were fast asleep.

We stood on the fountain's shore: woman + newborn.
We made one totem.
I named the baby *Easter Island.*

We played I spy.

I saw: Coins at the fountain's bottom. Eyes. Copper cataracts, winking through the water at us.
I held the baby close. I held the baby stiffly. I brought the baby to see nobody.

I saw: Statues in the fountain's water. Statues in tall grasses on the shore of a sea. I turned to tell somebody. The city had disappeared into complete silence. There was only: the baby.

We were watching the water wrinkle in the wind.
In the distance, maids were ironing.

Overhead, jets drew ciphers in the blue with their chalk.

The drift of the maker is dark.

Beware that by the drifts thou perish not.

The statues, the statues in the strange fountain were looking at us. They were weeping and turning, turning and weeping.

They might have seen the city shimmering in the sun and wind, and known... It was a city with no one in it. If a door somewhere on the street opened, it would always be... no one. It would be a bad draft that had blossomed.

I longed for meadows white with drifts of snow. I named the baby *Drift*.

In the winter I had planned to bring him north. To a barn's eaves, to hear icicles drip. To prepare him to grow up in the path of the next great glacial drift.

City whose sky was white jet streaks.

Whose houses were apparitions of asbestos flakes.

Whose homeless sipped wind from tins.

Whose only water was the strange fountain.

Angel, my angel, my sweetheart, wake up. See the foam on the wave, see the tornado, the hurricane.

We stood on the fountain's shore. The wind blew particulates of rug powder, of lemon-scented floor polish. The maids of the city were cleaning so completely. And mutely.

There may have been other names I gave the baby.

Zeno sweet Zeno

Little fellow little fellow

Vertigo

I said to the baby, We will stand here until there is snow on the mountain.

I may have meant to say *fountain*.

We peered all day into the strange fountain.

I said to myself, That is just your face stiffening around your cheeks. That is just grass growing at your feet.

I held the baby all the time, and he never ever cried.

THE JOB INTERVIEW

Actually, my current one—in the sacristy—is a good job.
And you know, it's *fulfilling*?

The pay isn't great, and I've had to make accommodations.
Bring a lunch and all. But if I forget my sandwich, there's always extra... bread lying around.

And wine.
Though on the job I would never!

Though, this is kind of gross, but—
I've acquired a bit of a taste for baptismal water.

After the water washes over the baby's forehead, you can't just dump it—
There's a special baptismal water sink, with a sacred drain.

Since it's so sacred—you know, the white lace, the whelp's skin—
Or maybe so dangerous—full of germs of original sin—

It seems a waste to put it down the drain.
So I've been sipping it.

Since I'm confessing, it'd probably be a stretch to say I only eat the communion
bread in emergencies, because I pretty much eat it all the time.

Though the incense under my arms was a singular occurrence.
I'd forgotten deodorant that morning, that's all.

That day, I may have performed my tasks in the sacristy a little more emphatically—
To, you know, get a little heat going under there.

The smell of the incense made me feel as if I were leading a solemn procession.
It also made me feel sort of sexy?

Anyway. I can't keep this job.
And I can't go back to the museum gig.

I mean, I still have the uniform and no one said anything *explicitly*
but after the incident with the Corot—

It was the Boatman of Montfortaine—
Have you ever seen it?

It's not even really my taste.
If I were going to get caught making out with a painting I'd rather have had it be a Basquiat.

But.

There was something about that picture. It has autumn in it.
Even though the trees aren't orange or brown.

Actually, the trees are greenish white. The sky is white.
Every time I'd look at it I'd feel white and blank.

And also the picture has this white and blank lake.
That I wanted to drink.

Later on, I did read about the pernicious effects of human saliva on paint.
It would be *terrible* to go back and see that I had caused any—

At one point, I also did some work as a skydiver.
It was a strange summer because I was pretty young and had just gotten my period.

Not to be gross, but I basically bled all summer. And that was mostly fine.
It was beautiful weather and I, you know, wore dark pants, took loads of baths.

But there was this one cloudy day, and they sent us up anyway.
I thought—if the crotch of my pants rubs against a cloud, I'll leave red streaks.

And I did fall through a cloudbank and even kind of tried to do a split mid-cloud.
But clouds are nothing to rub against, are nothing but emptiness.

I guess what I'm trying to say is that sky diving is still an option.

#1 I am not an idealist!
#2 I'll work anywhere and hard.

The thing with this sacristy job is—

The eating and drinking the bread and water is fulfilling
and I don't think anyone minds too much.

But part of the job is taking care of the vestments, and once a week you need to iron them.
And they're long—these long, white robes with 80 million folds.

And forget trying to do it on an ironing board.
So I've been using the altar, because it's really just the right length.

Something about pushing the iron back and forth—
All that cheap white cloth—

The altar has saints' bones buried inside it—
In the afternoon there's the stupid beautiful light through the stained glass—

I don't believe in God though. That's not where this is going.
Even if I believed *the Word became flesh*, well—

I'd probably just want to have sex with it.

Because there I was, just vestment ironing!
My mind was blank.

And the altar and the space were so majestic.
And the part of me that really responds to majesty are my hips.

So I was sort of rubbing myself against the altar.

And obviously, having an orgasm is antithetical to the whole spirit of the job.

I'm so sorry,
so sorry to have a body.

But how else.

I don't have heaven.
I don't have clouds even.

#3 What I'm really good at is loving this world well.

I just don't know who—
who I'm supposed to be or how to make enough money.

6: Do you eat meat?

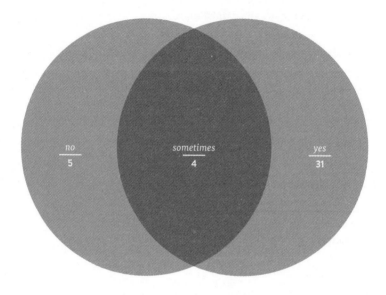

SANDRA DOLLER'S first book, *Oriflamme,* was published by Ahsahta Press in 2005. Her recent books include *Chora* (Ahsahta Press, 2010) and *Man Years* (Subito Press, 2011). Doller is the recipient of awards & fellowships including the Paul Engle–James Michener Fellowship, the Iowa Arts Fellowship, the PEN Writers Fund, and state arts grants from Iowa and Maryland. She completed her MFA from the Iowa Writers' Workshop in 2003 and her MA in Humanities from the University of Chicago in 2001. Doller is the founder & editrice of 1913 Press/1913 *a journal of forms* and assistant professor at California State University.

THE MERLESQUE

for Merle

[lessons]

*

This is my serpentine strip. It is not s-erpentine. It is serpent. It is strip of a strip from an unknown place. The lace is unknown. The p-lace is up north. On 37th Avenue. The place where the p-roject lives. Where the project no longer lives. The blue projector in the green brick place next to the electric green new wall on the metal rack. A rack that is not a rack but a shelf. A shelf without a self. A metal that is a wood. An unpainted wood near a newly painted wall. He will know what I am talking about. There is a strip in time. An animated film strip. Mine. There is a tennis court on the strip. A basket with not much. Now I am making this up. My strip has 4 bends. 8 sections that are 6 sections in the bend. The strip is a strip of strippiness. There are no strippy strippers. That's lies.

*

This rock is not made of choco. This choco is not made of bark. This choco bark is not edible. I will put this nowhere. Who owns this rock enough to carry it round in a tiny pocket. You do. You have eaten at the rock and called it din-din. I have a piece of bark in my eye. There it is. The wood that is at the bottom of every rock that is. Every rock that is not a wood rock comes from the wood. They might think we are joking. A bit of rock has brushed off onto my middle finger. I will not eat it. Hold it. I will not allow myself to eat this rock with you. I will not allow it. I will eat. I will call it chalk. Middle finger rock how do you do. I have a mossy underwear. Under there. Bananas.

*

General Sherman the pot smoking horse. Pony. General says My Little Pony. But the pony is not little. Then it is. He is. Pony for your thoughts. U.S. Pony have you a forelock that wanders, with a reputation for wandering, with a reputation? The pony should get shorter with time. Stupid pony bony. Aye. 7. I says the pony. I Seven. Several. Bothers. Orange pony ass. I have had enough of this pony. See, I wandered.

*

William in a skirt. Lying William. Pubic beard on William's face. Under William's skirt an egg, some tights, a dollar. William holds his hands like that forever. I have William's eyes. William wears a collar. Not the one you think. I have a need like William. Put your feet on the table, William, like a man do. Sleeveless William with ears and sensitive. William please pass me.

*

Eye drop. This is a black eye. Middle drop. Some objects are lines. Light blue task at the top. Drop. Playing with the back. Tight glossy back. Do you know what I am talking about, man? Rounder than a circle is the drop. Backer than the front. A belt with wings is not the drop. Why does it take so long to so long. A drop is worth a. Drop is worth.

*

I just touched lead. I think I just touched lead. I think there may be fluoride in there too. Do not touch lead, does not believe in evolution. This lead is giving me head. This lead is staying far away from me. It is my thing. This lead is a leader. A leader in the. Square apple apple monarch. Who has misread the leader this lead is. Someone took a picture of that. And wrapped it in lead, and wrapped it in lead, and wrapped it in the lead that I took. This lead will no have babies. Not have babies like I. I have decided to be done. I do not want to touch it no more. There is no narrative in this square.

*

Water over the greenness. There is a greenness with water insides. The greenness has smells. Smells like sneezes. Smells like buttons. Buttons has taken over talking. I think she will drink with anyone. There is a headache over thee coming on now from the greenness. First from the lead and now from the greenness. I will not transcribe this. I do not know where every thing comes from.

*

Up, pen. Up, dollar. Up your pen. Blue has recognized lead. This pen has no lead. I am sick sick of it. I am sick of making this pen my pen. I have a six-stomach question. From the time of the altering. There is a two. Line. Problem. A line problem? Is it "mine"? I am "confused."

*

Dual spot. Press & hold. Bye planet bike. Planet blike. Planet like. Like the light, lick the spot. Like. Wait. I am about to BE in here. Sick of the light, this light you wear, inside your mouth your problem. There is a big mouth problem there. I cannot stand the ~~sight~~ sound of it. I will like lick lack. Someday.

*

She was really writing there. About the National Archives Experience in Washington, D.C. She was writing so very really about the Experience with Elvis and Nixon and their hands, she was just writing it up about the Experience with Nixon and Elvis in the glove. Is it snowing up your globe? It is snowing up my globe. Did it snow up her globe? Is he laughing up his globe? He is shaking inside his globe, he is shaking hands. He is snakey shakey. There is a meal about it. A song. You stick to the picture. The Archive has its own globe and I am recording an ancient globy rhyme. The globe has globier parts and less globish or globular pieces. This is about that and not about this. This is how you make up a globe. With a pat of cold.

*

This makes it hungry. The pieces of dried It makes it hungrier yet. Apple peaches pumpkin pie. It is eyeing my hungrier colors. It is. It is made of leaf parts of animal fruits and dried parts and sticky features and the sketchiest natural bananas. It is made of smelly. Many people have tried to touch this here ocean. This box of goods. This chai-tastic. Children of the dried wonders. Its forest is hugely overrated. I am hoping I am not too too loud here.

*

What is coming my way, cha-cha? A smallish radio girl with here here feet. A painted petunia behind the ear. Her edges very colored. Almost outlined fluorescence topical. Wheels have to match the hair of It girl in radio. Here feet a carnation. Under each ear, an eye. A snobbish about girl children looking. Snub the wagon girl children lolling looging down nose at the grassy. Fluorescent grass child in the girl wagon snub child a fluorescent tint about reach extremity. Extremely. Tropics.

*

I recognize this man tool. The tool of mannish. Blue handled man. Stands. There is a current cross the X off the toolish. Do not look my page! I have the man tool too I know. The man tool has done it again. Yar. Rar. Says the man tool. I have a stunning lip. The man tool will fix it! I have a burning stomach. The man tool will fix it! I have a burning toe. The man tool! Tool! Too! I have a vein in my head that says "man." Boo.

7: What is your favorite journal or magazine?

1913
AGNI
A Public Space
Beloit Poetry Journal
Big Bell
Big Sky
Boston Review
Bright Pink Mosquito
Callaloo
Canary
Cave Wall
Cincinnati Review
Conduit x3
Court Green
Hambone
Hi-Fructose Magazine
Fence
Fou

GQ
JET
jubilat x3
Kenyon Review
London Review of Books
Longform
Love Is The Law
Lungfull!
Movement Research Journal
Ranger Rick, Jr.
River Styx
Rolling Stone
Poetry
The Dish (Andrew Sullivan)
The Nation x2
The New Yorker
The Volta
US Weekly

TIMOTHY DONNELLY

is the author of *Twenty-seven Props for a Production of Eine Lebenszeit* (Grove, 2003) and *The Cloud Corporation* (Wave, 2010), winner of the 2012 Kingsley Tufts Poetry Award. His poems have been widely anthologized and translated and they have appeared in such periodicals as *A Public Space, Fence, Harper's, The Iowa Review, jubilat, Lana Turner, The Nation, The New Republic, The Paris Review*, and elsewhere. He has served as poetry editor of *Boston Review* since 1996. He has been the Theodore H. Holmes '51 and Bernice Holmes Visiting Professor at Princeton University's Program in Creative Writing and Lewis Center for the Arts and is on the permanent faculty of the Writing Program at Columbia University's School of the Arts. He lives in Brooklyn with his wife and two daughters.

TO HIS DEBT

Where would I be without you, massive shadow
dressed in numbers, when without you there

behind me, I wouldn't be myself. What wealth
could ever offer loyalty like yours, my measurement,

my history, my backdrop against which every
coffee and kerplunk, when all the giddy whoring

around abroad and after the more money money
wants is among the first things you prevent.

My phantom, my crevasse—my emphatically
unfunny hippopotamus, you take my last red cent

and drag it down into the muck of you, my
sassafras, my Timbuktu, you who put the kibosh

on fine dining and home theater, dentistry and work
my head into a lather, throw my ever-beaten

back against a mattress of intractable topography
and chew. Make death with me: my sugar

boat set loose on caustic indigo, my circumstance
dissolving, even then—how could solvency

hope to come between us, when even when I dream
I awaken in an unmarked pocket of the earth

without you there—there you are, supernaturally
redoubling over my shoulder like the living

wage I never make, but whose image I will always
cling to in the negative, hanged up by the feet

among the mineral about me famished like a bat
whose custom it is to make much of my neck.

THE NEW INTELLIGENCE

After knowledge extinguished the last of the beautiful
fires our worship had failed to prolong, we walked
back home through pedestrian daylight, to a residence

humbler than the one left behind. A door without mystery,
a room without theme. For the hour that we spend
complacent at the window overlooking the garden,

we observe an arrangement in rust and gray-green,
a vagueness at the center whose slow, persistent
movements some sentence might explain if we had time

or strength for sentences. To admit that what falls
falls solitarily, lost in the permanent dusk of the particular.
That the mind that fear and disenchantment fatten

comes to boss the world around it, morbid as the damp-
fingered guest who rearranges the cheeses the minute the host
turns to fix her a cocktail. A disease of the will, the way

the false birch branches arch and interlace from which
hands dangle the last leaf-parchments and a very large array
of primitive bird-shapes. Their pasted feathers shake

in the aftermath of the nothing we will ever be content
to leave the way we found it. I love that about you.
I love that when I call you on the long drab days practicality

keeps one of us away from the other that I am calling
a person so beautiful to me that she has seen my awkwardness
on the actual sidewalk but she still answers anyway.

I say that when I fell you fell beside me and the concrete
refused to apologize. That a sparrow sat for a spell
on the windowsill today to communicate the new intelligence.

That the goal of objectivity depends upon one's faith
in the accuracy of one's perceptions, which is to say
a confidence in the purity of the perceiving instrument.

I won't be dying after all, not now, but will go on living dizzily
hereafter in reality, half-deaf to reality, in the room
perfumed by the fire that our inextinguishable will begins.

HIS FUTURE AS ATTILA THE HUN

But when I try to envision what it might be like to live
        detached from the circuitry that suffers me to crave

what I know I'll never need, or what I need but have
        in abundance already, I feel the cloud of food-court

breakfast loosen its embrace, I feel the shopping center
        drop as its escalator tenders me up to the story

intended for conference space. I feel my doubt diminish, my debt
        diminish; I feel a snow that falls on public statuary

doesn't do so sadly because it does so without profit.
        I feel less toxic. I feel the thought my only prospect

lies under a train for the coverage stop. Don't think I never
        thought that way because I have and do, all through

blank October a dollar in my pocket back and forth
        to university. Let the record not not show. I have

deserted me for what I lack and am not worth. All of this
        unfolds through episodes that pale as fast as others

gain from my inertia: I have watched, I'll keep watching
        out from under blankets as the days trip over the

days before out cold on the gold linoleum behind them
        where we make the others rich with sick persistence.

But when I try to envision what it might be like to change,
    I see three doors in front of me, and by implication

opportunity, rooms full of it as the mind itself is full
    thinking of a time before time was, or of the infinite

couch from which none part, and while the first two doors
    have their appeal, it's the third I like best, the one

behind which opens a meadow, vast, and in it, grazing
    on buttercups, an errant heifer with a wounded foot,

its bloody hoofprints followed by a curious shepherd back
    to something sharp in the grass, the point of a long

sword which, unearthed, the shepherd now polishes with
    his rodent-skin tunic, letting the Eurasian sun play

upon it for effect, a gift for me, a task, an instrument to lay
    waste to the empire now placed before me at my feet.

8: What is your favorite bookstore, and where is it located?

A used bookstore in Albany, NY

ADA Books, Providence, RI

Amherst Books, Amherst, MA

Black Sheep Books, Vancouver, BC

Book Court, Brooklyn, NY

Book Culture, New York, NY

Changing Hands, Tempe, AZ x2

City Lights, San Francisco, CA x3

Elliot Bay Books, Seattle, WA

Harvard Book Store, Cambridge, MA

Innisfree Poetry Bookstore, Boulder, CO

J. Hood Booksellers (formerly in Lawrence, KS, now online)

Kennys, Galway, Ireland

Kepler's, Menlo Park, CA

Left Bank Books, St. Louis, MO

Marfa Book Company, Marfa, TX

Micawbers Books, St. Paul, MN x2

Montclair Book Center, Montclair, NJ

Open Books, Seattle, WA

Open Source, Everywhere

Powell's Bookstore, Chicago, IL

Powell's Books, Portland, OR x3

Prairie Lights Books, Iowa City, IA x6

Second Story Books, Washington, DC

Seminary Co-Op, Chicago, IL x3

Shrine of the Black Madonna Bookstore, Atlanta, Houston, & Detroit

SPD, Oakland, CA

Tattered Cover, Denver, CO

The book swap at the Wellesley, MA Town Dump

The old Coliseum Books on 57th Street

Troubadour, Western MA x2

Unnameable Books, New York, NY

Woodland Pattern, Milwaukee, WI

JOSHUA EDWARDS
is the author of
Campeche (Noemi
Press, 2011) and
Imperial Nostalgias
(Ugly Duckling
Presse, 2013), and
the translator of
Mexican poet María
Baranda's *Ficticia*
(Shearsman Books,
2010). He's the
recipient of grants
and fellowships
from the Fulbright
Program, Vermont
Studio Center,
Zoland Poetry, Uni-
versity of Michigan,
Stanford University,
and the Akademie
Schloss Solitude,
and he was recently
selected as one of
the Poetry Society
of America's New
American Poets. He
directs and co-edits
Canarium Books.

DAYS OF DEATH

Love begins as dream and ends as rumor.
Will is a function of naïveté.
War is the mirror with a view of hell.
Government: a bridle on a dead horse.
Real estate, traffic, and relationships.
We are the teeth of a teeth-grinding world.
A bellybutton without a body.
Hope cranes its neck to have its head cut off.
Language is a houseplant in a motel.
Elephants have little use for aardvarks.
Posterity loves a kamikaze.
At midnight, the spine of daytime shivers.
Trained monsters are the most monstrous monsters.
Life dizzies air in the esophagus.
Property vomited monogamy.
Bird's nest, spider's web, man's unending wars.
The herd abstracts the individual.
For the nation, the world is abandoned.
Orphans remember what children forget.
The destructive sword shapes eternity.
A survivor is one who tortures death.
Man turns to face the wall he's backed against.
Civilization began in a gourd.
Aphorisms are the hangnails of thought.
Empathy begets pain through tolerance.
The soul hangs between lust and emptiness.
People of conviction are never free.
The stranger always moves further away.
Terror translates landscape into frontier.
Celebrity portends apocalypse.
A crucifix should weigh what a man weighs.

Heaven belongs to dying, not to death.
The world is post-unintelligible.
Memory encircles the past, then prods.
History shatters thought against language.
Chaos sends a formal invitation.
Every home hides a drawer full of knives.
Through poverty desire becomes darkness.
Child's play culminated in mushroom clouds.
Skepticism is merely consciousness.
When man kneels, God slips on a banana.
Beware of the priest with only one ear.
Tragedy folds fingers into a fist.
Dialectical day, critical night.
In pain, ownership is demystified.
All the best guard dogs bite before they bark.
Ag, bag, dwag, gwag, lag, mag, nag, rag, and swag.
Religion unearths the art of despair.
Age humbles even the cruelest genius.
Escape nostalgia by moving closer.
The wind in the trees, a Dorian mood.
Beauty and power strike the same poses.
Silk abstracted the flesh from history.
To become what one thinks, one must first lust.
Distance always subordinates the truth.
When belief doesn't narrow, it departs.
Darkness can only be seen from outside.
Empire is a country without nipples.
For the planet, volcano is a verb.
Music haunts the house of meaningfulness.
Spring's sweetness and the feast of its offices.
The weak in affection is strong in want.
As the sea and the snow double the sun.

Envy ultimately breeds addiction.
Only small islands are largely themselves.
Freedom must begin with vulgarity.
The eyes of love see Egypt from above.
Torment wears the mask of insanity.
Each new argument ages a nation.
When music plays, id grinds against ego.
Contradiction develops in exchange.
You can reject a thing and love it too.
Never mind stars, marvel at the darkness.
It rains until the cistern fills with spring.
There is nothing left to say about zoos.
Attempt to traverse until you collapse.
Love is a heaven full of misery.
Make of the dead your living vehicle.
From the heart's soft pipes gush the oils of war.
Never relinquish more than one delight.
To hurt someone is to beg them to heal.
All too familiar: success as failure.
Ecstasy expresses love's disclosure.
Ambition is not imagination.
Death has neither deadline nor duration.
Downhill is the sad reward for uphill.
In every man's mouth is a gate to hell.
Alienation belongs to us all.
The stars are around us, not above us.
A man's senses draw and quarter his heart.
A hand by itself is only one word.
Love *is* an and, it is not *of* an and.
Broken glass after the after party.
The observer's failure is called vision.
Saving angels, one's love will turn to dust.

The man is half the son his father was.
Shards of shattered glass or the world as-is.
Laughter in the bath before tears at sea.
Dying is treason against the body.
Beauty's shadow is also beautiful.

DISSIMILATIONS

You hold onto life like a hostage. You're deeply embedded.
You're an actor slipping into a new script. You're a comma
Whose purpose is to mark the moment when prose is suspended,
Where begins a poem's pensive silence or some dark drama.

You're a Charles Dickens character in the opium den
Of a long life. All you want is to sleep through the nights after
Satisfying intercourse, but your mimesis may have been
Caught by sexually transmitted diseases. Disaster

Is an evening when you're so hungry every apple core
Evokes grocery stores. Being the only one and only,
They can't clone or disown you. The only thing you lack is your
Adult teeth, beneath the rotten teeth of what makes you lonely.

And the truth is that devolution concurs with disposal
Till it emerges, when entourage lobbies for Decalogue,
And hype is the new preparation before its proposal,
Calling for the removal of all shoes, shirts, and demagogues,

And the zealous anti-Orientalists who refuse to
Use anyone's last names first when denying them service at
The sperm bank, where the preferred euphemism is "super glue."
Remember the joke about the butcher who couldn't get fat?

Rejuvenated vaginas and enhanced penises squeak
Thanks to Puritanism gone gaga vis-à-vis bling-bling
À la bada bing. People piled up form a sexual peak.
Two condoms put up their dukes inside a contraceptive ring.

Champagne is the new organizer for your political
Campaign to conceive something tantamount to FASD
Of the spirit. Were you surprised or did you wax critical
When you emerged from the driveway to your domesticity

Without any disease but your family's questionable
Cultural history? Is it such a mystery that your
Mediocrity's latently poised to emerge? That you're full
Of traditional vulnerability? You'll pace the floor

Until you face (at a number of paces proportional
To the gravity of the insults that have been thrown your way)
Yourself dressed like a clown. Your brain will halt to urbanely sprawl
And then catapult your past beyond your future like a clay

Pigeon across a clear blue sky, toward a lemonade stand
At which the theory of other minds attempts to explain
Why petroleum prices fluctuate with body count and
Meaningful relationships end in kaleidoscopic pain.

9: What's a word that you love?

About
Acetaminophen
Badelynge
Blues
Boulevard
Bowl
Bright
Brutal
Callipygian
Elegy
Fulcrum
Girl
Hasp
Idea
Labradoodle
Lattice
Lightning
Limerence
Love

Magnanimous
Maybe
Mojado
Mostacholi
Mouth
Of
Oilwell
Pleach
Poppycock
Pumpkin
Sacha
Samurai
Sandwich
Semaphore
Snood
That
Trounce
Trousers
Vetiver

ALL NATURAL
Dude
MAYONNAISE

EMILY KENDAL FREY
lives in Portland, Oregon, and teaches at Portland Community College and the Independent Publishing Resource Center. She is the author of several chapbooks and chapbook collaborations including, most recently, *Baguette* (Cash Machine, 2013). *The Grief Performance*, her first full-length collection, was published by Cleveland State University Poetry Center in 2011 and won the Norma Farber First Book Award from the Poetry Society of America in 2012.

KAABA/KISS THE STONE

1.

I take nothing and rub it hard

Last fuck for my palm

Genie in the lamp

The no of no, the no is nominal

I roll it between my fingers

I get it off

It gets me

Off

I trundle down to the railroad (tracks)

Oh the train is coming

Oh wait in bed

It's winter and the frost is forming

Dark-soft-cold

But for now pull the whistle in through the window

The one-celled nothing

The you float

The dish

The flat dish of puke

The plant, rotting by the window

The plant, dead on arrival

The water of birth

I wake to the cold moon

Above me, my mind thinks it is day

The frost shaking atop the neighbor's dog shit

The roses

Not dead yet

The dumb roses

2.

You are good with language

Let me say: binary

Let me rephrase: you have a set

A code

A black box

It detonates and dust settles

Dandruff

You write a letter to god

You delete it

Listen, I've got nothing but the teeth in my mouth

A door that sticks

I heave my car onto the freeway, out past the fields

The sun is up in a cotton sock sky

Weakly the planet hangs in place

The sun will say nothing

Shift no facts

I drive forward

My lungs

My dad

Kneeling in the strawberries out back

A tattoo of a reservoir

On my chest

3.

You circle around the box

You are eleven

There are nine of you

Each with eight arms

One head, viciously meticulous

One mouth for arranging

The eyes, red-rimmed

The child is crying

The sun refuses to move

4.

I came in through the front door

I am going to leave you I said

You looked like an old banana

Public

Shining death batter

Whipped in the bowl

You were making the percolator kind of coffee

You forgot the water

It burned on the stove

5.

I am sorry for my identity crisis

I thought it was your identity crisis but it was in fact mine

It's cool that you're all friends

Pig roast out back

Crack crack

I am sitting very still, now

We had moms

They were weird

We felt weird around her

And also at parties

When she was reading a book at home

10: What's a word that you hate?

Adjunct
Any abbreviation
Authentic
Behemoth
Classy
Community
Facebook
Fag
Fart
Flounce
Fun
Guesstimate
Hate
Impact
Impetus
Incentivize
Interesting
Lover *x2*

Master
Mayonnaise
Mealworm
Metadata
Oftentimes
Palimpsest
Panties
Pedagogy
Positionality
Post-black
Preggers
Pulchritude
Relatable
Rifle
Skeet
Slacks
Torque
Velvety

**DOBBY
GIBSON**
is the author of
three collec-
tions of poetry:
Polar (Alice
James Books,
2005), which
won the Bea-
trice Hawley
Award; *Skir-
mish* (Graywolf
Press, 2009);
and *It Becomes
You* (Graywolf
Press, 2013).
He lives in
Minneapolis.

SILLY STRING THEORY

My daughter's school roof softens,
dripping rain into the terrarium,
slowly drowning the snake.
Her ponytail, like the very filament of the universe,
won't stay bound long enough for lunch these days,
teaching me to age a little more gracefully
by teaching me to give in a little more gracefully,
just as one finally learns to find more pleasure
in tossing seeds on the happy couple
than in chasing bridesmaids with vodka tonics
hoping to liberate one from her catastrophe of satin.
Here's my number, a woman said to me
at a wedding many years ago,
handing over digits randomized to never connect us again,
which was like being given the combination
hidden at the heart of every galaxy,
the bingo balls of planets
being vacuumed into a black hole
like golf balls into the buggy
crisscrossing the driving range,
the one men and women older than mountains
smash each motherfucking 3-iron at.
The one piloted by a teenager
who is more or less exactly like I was at 17,
malformed and morosely mustached,
except he's four days from being worth a billion
for the website he built from ones and zeroes
to swap party pics, the one Proctor & Gamble
will use to sell us Crest White Strips.
Sorry, but the more invested I become in a subject,
the harder it is for me to define the subject.

Especially when Doc is up there on the roof
hacking another skin cancer from my scalp.
He started by jabbing a syringe
full of painkiller into the crown of my head,
which was, of course, exceptionally painful,
before it filled me with powers
I never knew I could posses:
the ability to head-butt a Buick,
speculate on the supersymmetry of bosons,
or successfully receive a left hook,
which any prize fighter will tell you
requires focus on the future, like winter coming,
the mall opening thirty minutes early
so the seniors can get their walk in without wiping out.
Like us, they always circle back
to talking about what ails them
and what their kids are up to these days,
the two subjects we all know the least about,
the storefronts shackled behind steel curtains,
the scent of yesterday's cinnamon buns in the air.

POLAR

Like the last light
spring snowfall
that seems to arrive
from out of nowhere
and not land, exactly, anyplace,
so too do the syllables of thought
dissolve silently into the solitude
of the body in thought.
Like touching your skin,
or the first time I touched ice
and learned it was really water
and that neither were glass,
so does the jet contrail overhead
zip something closed in us,
perhaps any notion of the bluer.
Glancing sunlight,
my shoulders bearing the burden
or any theory why these birds
remain so devoted
to their own vanishing.
One store promises flowers
for all your needs,
another tells you
everything must go.
One river runs like a wound
that will never heal,
one snow falls like a medicine
that will never salve,
you the Earth, me the moon,
a subject moved in a direction
you desire, but for reasons
I believe to be my own.

UPON DISCOVERING MY ENTIRE SOLUTION TO THE ATTAINMENT OF IMMORTALITY ERASED FROM THE BLACKBOARD EXCEPT THE WORD 'SAVE'

If you have seen the snow
somewhere slowly fall
on a bicycle,
then you understand
all beauty will be lost,
and how even that loss
can be beautiful.
And if you have looked
at a winter garden
and seen not a winter garden
but a meditation on shape,
then you know why
this season is not
known for its words,
the cold too much
about the slowing of matter,
not enough about the making of it.
So you are blessed
to forget this way:
a jump rope in the ice melt,
a mitten that has lost its hand,
a sun that shines
as if it doesn't mean it.
And if in another season
you see a beautiful woman
use her bare hands
to smooth wrinkles
from her expensive dress
for the sake of dignity,
but in so doing trace

the outlines of her thighs,
then you will remember
surprise assumes a space
that has first been forgotten,
especially here, where we
rarely speak of it,
where we walk out onto the roofs
of frozen lakes
simply because we're stunned
we really can.

WHAT IT FEELS LIKE TO BE THIS TALL

Not one of my costumes is believable.
I'm constantly away on business.
The morning, chiropractic, saddles me
beneath its colossal gravity.
In search of a breath, kneeling at the shallows,
the minnows scatter.
Wind farms hum atop the prairie.
Wilt Chamberlain's bones groan from their earthen locker.
In my most private thoughts,
radio signals from distant lands
argue invisibly over static,
and like an ice-cream headache,
the only thing worse than feeling this way
is not having a reason to feel this way,
hoping against hope, against nature,
versus self — I miss you all so much. Send money!
I don't have a fight song,
yet isn't that alone reason enough to fight?
Let the academics roll their eyes.
Faced with a progressively larger fork
for every subsequent course,
at some point, even my belongings began to mock me.
I couldn't eat another bite.
I'm starving.
Whatever you love most
is just another thing for me to bonk my head on.
I can't even trust a kite.
Above the rest of you, from the back row
of my second-grade class photo,
Kristin Dahlberg and I could see giraffes migrate the Serengeti.
Our knees ached with empathy.

Their hearts were as big as basketballs.
Tribal drums called us from the distance.
The distance called us from the distance.
Soon, everything would get knocked over,
and yet we would come in peace.

YONA
HARVEY

is a literary artist
living in Pittsburgh,
Pennsylvania. She
is the author of
the poetry col-
lection *Hemming
the Water* (Four
Way Books: New
York, 2013) and the
recipient of an Indi-
vidual Artist Grant
from the Pittsburgh
Foundation. She
also enjoys explor-
ing and reading
about the neighbor-
hood streets where
jazz pianist and
composer Mary Lou
Williams grew up.
Williams married
the spiritual to the
secular in her mu-
sic, and is a regular
muse in Yona's
writing. For more
information visit
yonaharvey.com.

SOUND—PART 1 (GIRL WITH RED SCARF)

There was a girl with a red scarf, a girl with a white scarf, a girl with a pink scarf, & a girl with a scarf of pale pale blue. & when, from a corner of earth, far from where the girls were born, & far from where any of the girls then stood, their scarves unwound & snapped like ribbons or wild wild hair, it was the girl with the red scarf who stood apart from the others, though they all stood laughing wildly together. & there was talk of toads, & talk of kissing, & many gowns & much ceremony, but mostly talk for talk's sake away from too many ears curved to listen. Though listening is what the girl with the red scarf did most, which made her from a distance seem still, though she moved with the other girls or at other times with her brothers & sisters in a queue slithering onto the school bus or into the house, which was never still. & when at particular moments her ears were full of odd instructions, & she needed to hear something across a room, she listened with the whole of her body, her eyes & skin, her hair, which was not wild but microscopically braided. Sound was God, as she understood it, always poised to listen. What does a girl with a red scarf hear? Only she knows, approaching the world from the inside in. The center of the ear: a drum. Rain on leaves. Fingers on books. On bellies. On windows. With a boy pressed against her, she attempted music, a collaborative first. An unsex. What was that sound? The naught-girl signal? Womanish gardenia opening? God is good. (Sometimes). Fierce fragmentation, lonely tune.

TO DESCRIBE MY BODY WALKING

To describe my body walking I must go back
to my mother's body walking with an aimless switch
in this moment of baptismal snow or abysmal flurry.
There's a shadow of free-fall frenzy & she unhurried

the way snowflakes are unhurried toward transformation
at my living room window. She moves unlabored, she
will not ask me to invite her in, but she will expect it.

I will open the door to her. She is my mother,
even if she is made of snow & ice & air & the repetition
of years. (A means, a ways).
She came out of trees surrounding me. I see her cross

now the creek in her patent leather shoes, their navy
glimmer like a slick hole I might peer over & fall into,
against so much snow weighing down the prayerful arms

of sycamores, which doused the bushes last autumn.
Her little hearse broke down near the exit
that leads to my house. Now she must walk.
She will be tired. I will let her in,

though she will not ask. She has come so far
past the mud & twigs, the abandoned nests.
This time of year she can't tell the living from the dead.

The pathway is mostly still except for her moving
with the snow, becoming the snow. Forgiveness?
She is a stamp in it, the tapping of boots
at the porch steps.   Not spring.

Or summer. Just her advancing, multiplying—
    —falling through branches
        —there's a flurry of her.

MOTHER, LOVE

Because you are not April or June or January or
slush-caked boots or snow falling or melting or moving
in from the north west plains, one cold coffee of a late

night, my bruise, my blade, my thorn, I love. Here

in the fold of a cramped journal, I've nothing
to whine about, to hate, or to feel indifferent to.
I write with the ink that is your name, dark

blood in the droop of a pale handkerchief.

When the baker runs her hands against the smooth
flour & sugar tins with their satisfied lids she is
not like you. She is not your sewing

machine in danger of falling over the edge. No,

you're at least thirteen clocks in the span
of two rooms, each off by a minute or two.
Lord, help me when they chimed.

& so my love is awkward & ill-timed.

Here's the oversized window you
keep looking out of.
What trip are you planning, you

never punctual retired secretary, you
flat-ended film, you holy shock of self-absorption,
polyester panties, cotton knit pajamas, you

paper jam, you yesterday, you
Minister of Excuses, you tardy bell,
parcel package, unexpected visitor,
unanswered phone call, shout
from the basement, rainstorm,
static in the busted speaker, hearing
aid, headache, cabinet void of teabags
& measuring cups, passive-aggressive,
stomach ache, one & a half minutes too long, day
late, dollar short mother
of mothers, you
mother
you.

STEVE HEALEY is the author of two books of poetry, *Earthling* (2004) and *10 Mississippi* (2010), both published by Coffee House Press. His poems have appeared in anthologies such as *Legitimate Dangers: American Poets of the New Century,* and in many journals, such as *American Poetry Review, Boston Review, Fence,* and *jubilat.* His essays and criticism have appeared in magazines such as the *Writer's Chronicle* and *Rain Taxi.*

TERMINAL MORAINE

Midway on our journey we'd gotten lost like golfballs
in a dark forest. Like tiny brains shanked into the unknown
by a slippery three-wood, we'd forgotten why
we were supposed to keep score. One of us said,
up ahead there's a new path, let's give up the old path.
Soon the new path began to look like the old path in reverse,
and we kept feeling that old loss of newness.
Someone said that we were lost on the geological debris
left behind by a glacier 10,000 years ago,
midway on its journey back home. Someone recalled
getting lost once in a photobooth on a beach in New Jersey.
Someone recalled getting lost once in a bumblebee costume.
Someone said that researchers had put some ants
on stilts and cut the legs of other ants in half
to prove that ants find their way home by counting steps.
We'd lost count long ago, but then someone recalled
a small green pond at the start of our journey and said,
we should start thinking like a pond. The pond appeared
and said, this is the end of the path, you should start
thinking like a fire. Already we could see the burning wood,
and the trees all around, the not-burning trees,
watching the fire with awe. Someone said,
if you look far enough into the fire you can see
the embers flashing like a tiny chorus line.
Someone said, if you look far enough into the stars,
you can see a limousine pulling up, ready to drive us
into morning. The pond said, listen to these kick-ass frogs,
they remember what the glacier felt like when
it retreated, like it was letting go of a book
it would never finish. We listened to the frogs,
and for a while, we didn't say anything stupid.

ALL UMBRELLAS COME FROM FIRE

> *All flus come from China.*
> —Dobby Gibson, "Fumage"

> *Only you can prevent forest fires.*
> —United States Forest Service

"Fumage" is a word that sounds French
and means "Smokey the Bear."
Fear of fire comes from the intense desire
to make fire. Thus, Wolfgang Paalen
invented fumage by drawing figures
on paper with the smoke from a candle.
They are sooty, savage humans
with sausagey limbs, dancing like bears.
Many bears are called "fumage"
because of the funny way they dance,
but only Smokey wears pants.
What's the function of those pants?
Only you know the answer.
The word "fumage" also refers to smoking,
as in smoked fish, and of course bears
are known to dance in exchange
for sardine treats. They participate
in an economy driven by scarcity.
Only you have what I want.
Each genus is divided into species.
All Panda bears come from China
and are stuffed with flammable stuffing.
All stuffing comes from dreams.
All truths come from the flu,
curled up in bed in the shape of a moan.
When you look out a window at 2:47 a.m.

and the neighbor's garage is on fire,
it feels like you did it. Only you
are a pyro. Or a little after noon,
the sun pressing down on your neck
like a forest fire, and the angular shadow
that slips under your shoe each time
you place it a little farther up the sidewalk
is the one thing that comes from you.
It is your only idea, and if you
look away, it doesn't exist,
there is no idea that we come from
the smoke of a candle. And yet we know
that all umbrellas come from China,
and when it begins to rain there,
we open our umbrellas here.

ESSAY ON THE BOY WE ALMOST RAN OVER

We almost accidentally ran over a little boy in the parking lot.
We hadn't expected anything terrible to almost happen when backing out.
It was a nice day and we'd just had a nice time at the lake when

we almost accidentally ran over a little boy in the parking lot.
The radio was on and we weren't paying attention when we backed out.
On the radio someone said the plan to raise taxes was dead in the water.

It was a nice day and we'd just had a nice time at the lake when
we heard a little boy make the sound of almost being run over by a car.
There was a long moment of not understanding anything because

on the radio someone said the plan to raise taxes was dead in the water,
but then we looked and saw the little boy and began to understand.
He ran to his parents and they yelled at him for being careless.

There was a long moment of not understanding anything because
he was already so scared, then his face fell apart and he cried.
It happened in the United States in a terrible parking lot where

he ran to his parents and they yelled at him for being careless.
We began to drive again, we couldn't imagine doing anything else,
and we wanted to drive into the future and try not remembering that

it happened in the United States in a terrible parking lot where
we easily could have killed a little boy with our new eco-friendly car.
The sound of fender hitting his torso, his head hitting pavement,

and we wanted to drive into the future and try not remembering that
we'd had such a nice time floating in the water like drowned people,
and we lived in the United States of not having to say goodbye to

the sound of fender hitting his torso, his head hitting pavement.

Steve Healey   151

11: *What genre do you read the most?*

Books About Teaching
Email
Essays
Fantasy
Fiction x8
Genre
How-To
Job Advertisements
Journalism
Mystery
Movies
Nonfiction x5
Philosophy
Poetry x14
Poetry Criticism
Pop Psychology
Prose
Prose Poetry
Really Thick Novels
Science
Sci-Fi
Short Fiction x2
Snark
Teacher-Parent Updates
The Genre of the Dark-Yet-Fancily-Dressed

TYEHIMBA JESS'S first book of poetry, *leadbelly*, was a winner of the 2004 National Poetry Series. A Cave Canem and NYU alumni, he received a 2004 Literature Fellowship from the National Endowment for the Arts, and was a 2004–2005 Winter Fellow at the Provincetown Fine Arts Work Center. Jess was a 2006 Whiting Fellowship recipient. He exhibited his poetry at the 2011 TedX Nashville Conference. He is an assistant professor of English at the College of Staten Island.

COON SONGS MUST GO! COON SONGS GO ON...(1)

A show goes	*all 'cross country,*
to a	*farmland*
country town	*or big city -*
- some low down	*uppity Negroes put*
loudmouth	*blame on a*
coon shouter	*minstrel for how he*
sings	*moanin'*

"Coon, Coon, Coon"

or some other song	*- but we wear blackface*
that has plenty of coon in it	*to make white folks' truths easier,*
with an emphasis on the word coon.	*to mask the ugly in their mirrors.*

Left side is excerpted from "Coon Songs Must Go!" Indianapolis Freedman, Jan. 2, 1909

GENERAL BETHUNE V. W.C. HANDY* 1885

Blind, half-crazy, or illiterate: this
mastermind of piano - he's a goldmine.
But Lord, he's a demon when he gets his
blood all hot. Tom's got to be feelin' high
if he's going to bring the music to life.
He'll stomp the ground and cry like a child-
and won't stop till he gets his way. He'll give strife
to anyone who plays his songs wrong. Like
when he pushed that off-tune girl off his stool
-he cursed her hard. And he's been known to strike
folk who play his songs clumsily. See, fools
get God's grace, just like a child. He just might
earn twenty thousand blessed bucks per tour
-minus management and upkeep fees, of course

Ol' Blind Tom must be some great Hoodoo
of sound workin' them keys. He's got that mojo-
magic hard. Gets some whites steamed, boils their blued
spirits cause he don't care 'bout 'fending folks
-he got a strong conjure on him. I hear
that he'll talk back to a white man all day –
to no-talent white women, too – I mean,
they say that blind boy got crackers all scared
and warned against messin' up his music
-no, he don't take kindly to no tone deaf
with dumb hands – he shucks em'. But watch - Tom will
make a handsome sum for somebody, I bet-
and maybe they let him save some of that dough
- enough to send pennies to mama back home...

*W.C. Handy met Blind Tom as a youth. General Bethune was Blind Tom's master and manager.

GENERAL JAMES BETHUNE AND JOHN BETHUNE INTRODUCE BLIND TOM

Here he is, the Amazing Blind Tom....
he's pitched in darkness, exalted through sound   he's mastered sharp and flat of piano:
                                        a slave whose head is a trunk full of song
pealing from each deft fingertip. We've found   a musical freak, a brown tornado,
                        a maestro who conjures three tunes at once-
a storm that brings lightning, thunder and rain   a far cry from the fields his kin slaved, he's
                        like a one man band. This chattel's become
        filled with the light of music. His brain's   besotted with syncopation. He seems
                        unlocked by 88 keys to sing out
        jingling with joy, the way an angel gets   blessed in the thrall of some idiot god
                        raptured into tongues. Tom is, beyond doubt,
winged past sorrow, each note pulled from his head   sprung from some holy, dark place that got
                        burnished by fate and delivered by songs
                We present to you Mr. Wiggins - Ol' Blind Tom....

MARK TWAIN** V. BLIND TOM*

Some archangel,   I'm sent from above-
cast out of upper Heaven   like rain on blue prayers.
like another Satan,   blessed with Gabriel's lost notes, I
inhabits this coarse casket;   can see up to God's throne, yes,
and he comforts himself   while he plays this soul
and makes his prison   of flesh free- makes me
beautiful with   the music of piano, the
thoughts and   breath and
dreams and   burn in the
memories of   stormcloud's roar from
another time   when sound called up,
and another existence   first made me whole.
that fire   sounds like *love*.
this dull clod   weighted in my chest
with impulses and inspirations   -it finds freedom after
it no more comprehends   hurt. I hear Earth's tremble harsher
than does the stupid worm   -better than the soil itself. When
the stirring of the spirit within   land and tree sing to me, I hear
her   notes
of the   wildly
gorgeous captive   blooming inside- a spirit
whose wings she   shadows across my face,
fetters   breaking free
and   unloosed. I play the wind
whose flight she stays   in my blood.

** Left side is original quote from Mark Twain's Special Letters to the *San Francisco Alta California* August 1, 1869

*Blind Tom was a highly popular autistic and blind pianist who performed throughout the US from 1860's until his death in 1908

BLIND TOM: ONE BODY, TWO GRAVES BROOKLYN/GEORGIA*

Here I lie, Blind Tom: Piano Man. I'm free

here in Brooklyn soil, I'm 'mancipated-   like so much Georgia dust; I rest quiet -

    like lightnin' bugs ghostin' up night. And now I can see-

at last! I watch each piano's breath baited   beneath pinetop and cedar. I feel God's riot

    beneath each finger that seeks to strike a key in the key

    of wonder. I conjure a claim   of birdsongs blended from each season's sun

        rooted deep in black muscle memory

that's set slaves almost free, that carved its name   scrawling across each heart, the music's brunt

        ringing like a bell, like an open wound

thick as thunder through city summer air-   shimmering all over the country's soul-

    from mouths that bend flattened dreams into tune-

I'm nowhere at all, but sing everywhere-   I dance inside each holla and whole note -

    Let me introduce to those who ain't heard me:

    Here I am, Blind Tom: Piano Man. Free.

*Blind Tom was buried first in Brooklyn's Greenpoint Cemetery, and then allegedly moved by the Bethune family to Columbus, GA. However, records in Brooklyn indicate the body was never moved. There are headstones in both states for Blind Tom. This syncopated sonnet may be read line by line, forwards, backwards, and interstitially.

KEETJE KUIPERS has been the Margery Davis Boyden Wilderness Writing Resident, and a Wallace Stegner Fellow at Stanford University. Her first book, *Beautiful in the Mouth*, was published in 2010, and her second book, *The Keys to the Jail*, is forthcoming. Keetje was most recently the Emerging Writer Lecturer at Gettysburg College, and is now an assistant professor at Auburn University.

BONDAGE PLAY AS A SUBSTITUTE FOR PRAYER

Slack bodies need a chain, a tightening.

Because I have a good life,
because the scales are tipped too far
toward my own contentment, I ask my man
to put his hands around my wicker throat
and squeeze. I'm familiar with the consequences
of happiness: When we become too easy in our lives,
god doesn't waste his time making an example of us.
Better that I take my beating from a hand
I love. When beauty and pleasure cling
to my staticed legs, when fortune's grotesque
and comely filaments cloud my hair,
I know to ask for pain.   Without the wick of wire,
I fear god-on-earth, his deep hands churning
through the most tender porches of my body,
the shadows he commands my fine rails
cast. I'll take my punishment from my man
or this bed becomes my unlacquered black ocean,
my bottomless potato field, my factory floor
where unseen hands hold me down,
my church where I can't even say, *yes, hit me.*

There's only so much goodness one body can hold.

ACROSS A GREAT WILDERNESS WITHOUT YOU

The deer come out in the evening.
God bless them for not judging me,
I'm drunk. I stand on the porch in my bathrobe
and make strange noises at them—

                         language,

if language can be a kind of crying.
The tin cans scattered in the meadow glow,
each bullet hole suffused with moon,
like the platinum thread beyond them
where the river runs the length of the valley.
That's where the fish are.

                     Tomorrow

I'll scoop them from the pockets of graveled
stone beneath the bank, their bodies
desperately alive when I hold them in my hands,
the way prayers become more hopeless
when uttered aloud.

                  The phone's disconnected.

Just as well, I've got nothing to tell you:
I won't go inside where the bats dip and swarm
over my bed. It's the sound of them
shouldering against each other that terrifies me,
as if it might hurt to brush across another being's
living flesh.

            But I carry a gun now. I've cut down
a tree. You wouldn't recognize me in town—
my hands lost in my pockets, two disabused tools
I've retired from their life of touching you.

DROUGHT

The last days of dandelions—even the dog's gone
to fluff. And those flowers that smell like semen,
like alcohol and sugar swirled under my nose. I'm so

thirsty I could cry. What's the name for those bugs
that bat against any lit window? I stumble around
my dim furniture just to keep them away. I'm not sure

I could stand their need. Heat lightning is all I have
coming to me: its silence, its lie. Some nights
I go outside and pretend I can feel water on my face,

imagine it draining down to the aquifer, changing
the shape of the darkness that's been sitting there
all along. I'll shoot out the street light if I have to.

THE KEYS TO THE JAIL

It's the second day of spring.
In Montana, we burn our garbage.
Two blocks down, the Dairy Queen
swings open its shutters for another
season. We tell our sad stories
until the dog hangs his head
in the wet snow-wells of the too-soon
tulips. It gets uglier every year:
The same melt that clears the gutters
uncovers the dead, or the not-dead-
long-enough. And suddenly
we smell them again, their bodies
unlocked from that frozen state
of decay, mouths slack
but whispering, their cold breath
fresh on the air. Except the breath
is our own, the voices belong
to you and me, and the music they make
is not the swift tumble of locks,
but the soft drop of bones in a bowl.

12: What movie would you bring to a desert island?

Annie Hall	My son laughing
Bananas	Orphee
Broadway Danny Rose	Paris is Burning
City Lights (Charlie Chaplin)	Paris, TX x2
Contact	Poldark
Cool Hand Luke	Purple Rain
Crimes & Misdemeanors	Rust and Bone
Do The Right Thing	Satantango (Bela Tarr)
El Topo	Spirited Away
Eternal Sunshine of the Spotless Mind	Stalker (Tarkovsky)
Fata Morgana	The Big Lebowski
Gummo	The Godfather
Henry Fool	The Muppet Movie
Golden Girls DVDs	The Shining
Gosford Park	The Tempest
I Do Not Know What It Is I Am Like	Through a Glass, Darkly
Kill Bill	Tout Va Bien
Mary Poppins x2	Umberto D.
Mulholland Drive	When We Were Kings

**NICK
LANTZ**
is the author of
*We Don't Know
We Don't Know*
(Graywolf Press)
and *The Lightning
That Strikes the
Neighbors' House*
(University of Wis-
consin Press). His
third book, *How to
Dance as the Roof
Caves In,* is due out
from Graywolf in
2014. Lantz earned
his MFA from
the University of
Wisconsin–Madi-
son, has received
fellowships from
the Wisconsin
Institute for Crea-
tive Writing and
the Bread Loaf
Writers' Confer-
ence, and was an
Emerging Writer
Lecturer at Gettys-
burg College.

PORTMANTERRORISM

Would it make a difference to say we suffered
from affluenza in those days? Could we blame
Reaganomics, advertainment, the turducken
and televangelism we swallowed by the sporkful,
all that brunch and jazzercise, frappuccinos
we guzzled on the Seatac tarmac, sexcellent
celebutantes we ogled with camcorders while
our imagineers simulcast the administrivia
of our alarmaggedon across the glocal village?
Would it help to say that we misunderestimated
the effects of Frankenfood and mutagenic smog,
to speculate that amid all our infornography
and anticipointment, some crisitunity slumbered
unnoticed in a roadside motel? Does it count
for nothing that we are now willing to admit
that the animatronic monster slouching across
the soundstage of our tragicomic docusoap
was only a distraction? Because now, for all our
gerrymandering, the anecdata won't line up for us.
When we saw those contrails cleaving the sky
above us, we couldn't make out their beginning
or their end. What, in those long hours of ash,
could our appletinis tell us of good or of evil?

THE MIRACLE

Around the small stone footprint, we built a temple.
          Each new autumn the seedpods
                    split open as before.
No one living today remembers the miracle.

          In the story, God doles out
               duties to each new creature,
but when humans arrive he has nothing left to give.
          Not every stutter
               in the genome is a miracle.

Outside the temple, the statue of a horse weeps all day.
          In each loaf we found a mouse
               baked hard as a peach stone.
Onto their alms bowls, the saints carved the word *miracle*.

          Every spring we took the strongest
               man in the village
and nailed him to a tree. We paid three women to grieve.
          What other animal hungers
               for such miracles?

The saints once carried around homilies heavy as bricks:
          always beat the beaten dog
               that comes back to you.
Each house we built during those years was a miracle.

          When struck, the statue's limbs
               yield different notes.
The blind man carves thirty soapstone birds every day,
          each bird more misshapen,
               each one named Miracle.

"OF THE PARRAT AND OTHER BIRDS THAT CAN SPEAKE"

It is for certain knowne that they have died for very anger and griefe
that they could not learn to pronounce some hard words.
—Pliny the Elder

When you buy the bird for your mother
you hope it will talk to her. But weeks pass
before it does anything except pluck the bars
with its beak. Then one day it says, "infect."

Your mother tells you this on the phone,
and you drive over, find the frozen meals
you bought for her last week sweating
on the countertop. "In fact," she says

in answer to your question, "I *have* been
eating," and it's as you point to the empty
trash can, the spotless dishes, that you
realize the bird is only saying, "in fact,"

that this is now the preamble to all
of your mother's lies. "In fact," she says,
"I have been paying the bills," and you
believe her until you find a cache

of unopened envelopes in the freezer.
More things are showing up where
they shouldn't. Looking out the back
window one evening you see craters

in her yard. While she's watching TV,
you go out with a trowel and excavate
picture frames, flatware that looks like
the silver bones of some exquisite

animal. You worry when you arrive
one day and see the open, empty cage
that you will find the bird dead, stuffed
in an oven mitt and left in a drawer,

but you find it sitting on her shoulder
in the kitchen. "In fact," she says,
"he learned to open the cage himself."
The bird learns new words. You learn

which lies you can ignore. The stroke
that kills her gives no warning, not—
the doctor assures you—that anyone
can predict such things. When you

drive home that night with the cage
belted into the passenger seat, the bird
makes a sound that is not a word
but that you immediately recognize

as the sound of your mother's phone
ringing, and you know it is the sound
of you calling her again and again,
the sound of her not answering.

MUTTON

A dark strip club—oh how dark. The low stage thrusts out. At its end, a vertical pole. And wolves. Wolves at the bar, wolves in dark suits at the heart-shaped tables. Garish music: techno, electronic drum beat like tooth on bone amplified. Too loud to think. The wolves drink. The wolves talk in underwater voices. Now and then a laugh like a puncture wound. Over crackly speakers, an announcer, his enthusiasm practiced, a barbed fishhook.

ANNOUNCER: All right, fellas, the moment you've been waiting for. Making her debut at Mutton tonight...Little Avery!

Music changes, quieter, more of a slow thump now, someone locked in a trunk, kicking. Light the color of viscera. Little Avery, a ewe, enters. A few disinterested glances tossed her way. She holds a pair of electric shears, trailing a long extension cord. Once on stage, she dances (gyrating, rubbing up against the pole, etc.).

ANNOUNCER: Come on! Let's see it! Don't you boys want to see it? *(etc., ad lib)*

After a hesitation, Avery switches on the electric shears, their hornet whine clear over the music. A few wolves glance up, then go back to their drinks. Avery begins to shave the wool off her body, small patches at a time. A lone dollar bill lands on the stage, like a disinterested housefly. Nothing more. She continues.

ANNOUNCER: Oh yes! Fellas, ain't she a sweet young thing? *(etc., ad lib)*

A wolf rises, crosses, Avery watching. He passes the stage, passes her, goes to the buffet, fills up a plate with hot wings, returns to his seat.

ANNOUNCER: Here we go, boys! This is it! *(etc., ad lib)*

Avery finishes shaving. Everything is gone. The sheers stop whining. Someone looks up, coughs. The song turns over like a bad dream. Avery retrieves the single bill, exits.

END

13: Where's a place you've never been to that you'd like to visit?

A desert island

Alaska

Antarctica

Argentina

Barcelona

Chichen Itza

Eden

Florence

Greenland

Heaven

Hong Kong

India *x2*

In n' Out Burger

Inside of Fort Knox

Istanbul, Turkey

Japan *x3*

Kauai

Lagos

Legoland in Denmark

Machu Picchu

Madison, WI

Mexico

Mont Joli, Quebec

Moon

Morocco

Naples

Narnia

My son's future

Outer space

Patagonia

Rome

Russia

Spain

St. Petersburg

Rainer Maria Rilke's brain synapses

The Red Sea

The Wall of China

Vancouver

**DOROTHEA
LASKY**

is the author of
AWE, *Black Life*, and
Thunderbird, all from
Wave Books. She is
also the author of
several chapbooks
and poem–picture
books, including
Poetry Is Not a Project
(Ugly Duckling
Presse, 2010). Her
work has been
included in *The
Paris Review*, *The New
Yorker*, *Boston Review*,
and *American Poetry
Review*, among other
places. She has been
educated at University of Pennsylvania,
Harvard University,
University of Massachusetts Amherst,
and Washington
University. She currently lives in New
York City and can
be found online at
birdinsnow.com.

BABY OF AIR

Baby of air
You rose into the mystical
Side of things
You could no longer live with us
We put you in a little home
Where they shut and locked the door
And at night
You blew out
And went wandering through the sea and sand
People cannot keep air in
I blow air in
I cannot keep it in
I read you a poem once
And you called it beauty
And then I read you another one and
You called it harmony air
My brother is not air, he is water
He is not a baby, he is older than me
And when he brushes the hair from my face
I cannot see him, but he surrounds me
I cannot see you baby of air
I put you in your bed and you get out
I put you in the air and you blend
I put you on the beach and you blow out
Like an air bird, flying and flying
I find other things similar to you
And like you, they are air and
Are nothing eventually
I am not made out of air
I hold your baby body in me
As I am a mother to you

I am a mother to you
My brother is my mother
He tells me when I have lost you
To grieve grieve
He says grieving is good
He says crying is good
He says sadness hits you in waves
Of water and air
I feel your fine hair hit me when I am sleeping
I feel your hair hit me in the head
Will you remember me
When you breeze upon the other world
O you are already there
O you are already there
My brother tells me, you are already there
He is already there, he says
And I cry
And he tells me
It is ok to cry
It is ok to cry,
He says
You are not made of air
It is ok to cry, he says
When you are not made of air

I LIKE WEIRD ASS HIPPIES

I like weird ass hippies
And men with hairy backs
And small green animals
And organic milk
And chickens that hatch
Out of farms in Vermont
I like weird ass stuff
When we reach the other world
We will all be hippies
I like your weird ass spirit stick that you carry around
I like when you rub sage on my door
I like the lamb's blood you throw on my face
I like heaping sugar in a jar and saying a prayer
And then having it work
I like cursing out an enemy
And then cursing them in objects
Soaking their baby tooth in oil
Lighting it on fire with a tiny plastic horse
I like running through the fields of green
I am so caught up in flowers and fruit
I like shampooing my body
In strange potions you bought wholesale in Guatemala
I like when you rub your patchouli on me
And tell me I'm a man
I am a fucking man
A weird ass fucking man
If I didn't know any better I'd think I were Jesus or something
If I didn't know any better I'd sail to Ancient Greece
Wear sandals
Then go to Rome
Murder my daughter in front of the gods

Smoke powdered lapis
Carve pictographs into your dress
A thousand miles away from anything
When I die I will be a strange fucking hippie
And so will you
So will you
So get your cut-up heart away from
What you think you know
You know, we are all going away from here
At least have some human patience
For what lies on the other side

I HAD A MAN

Today when I was walking
I had a man tell me as he passed
That I was a white bitch (he was white)
And to not look at him
Or he was going to 'fuck me in my little butthole'
I wandered away
Who is to say
I think I am a white bitch
My butt is big
But I believe my butthole is little
This violence that we put on women
I don't think it's crazy
Someone I know said
'Oh, that man was crazy'
I don't think he was crazy
Maybe he could tell I had a look in my eye
That wasn't crazy anymore
Maybe he could feel the wild cool blood in me
And it frightened him
Maybe he knew I was the same as him
But had been born with this kind face and eyes
Doughlike appurtenances
What about the day I left
What happened then
Large dark bird barreling down upon me
In the gentle air, to take me in his beak
Pink and patterned house
Neverending sister speech
To go along the coaster and never return
To never repeat
Did that one bitter eye know I have a voice

To say what my words have done to me
That unkind wind that blew thru my brain
With no thought of me
Just to still the jungle animals
Just to feed the endless clearing
The giant
Green and simple
Face of the sea

TORNADO

I remember he was bent down
Like a whirlpool
I was yelling at him
He looked scared and backed away
Another time, I squinted my eyes to see
And he said I looked ugly
The funny part was when
My sister asked me where he went to
And I just didn't know
He just disappeared one day into nothing
I am rotting and rancid
Each day, rotting, but I am water, too
I am a watery nymph that is hot and wet
Like a wetted beast
I saw the man walking, hunched over
And thought it was him
"Father!" I yelled after the man
Who was hunched, he was going somewhere
He turned but the face was green
It is a black life, but I don't want to die
I don't want to die, I don't ever want to die
Goddamn you, don't you shoot me in my sleep
Let me rot on this earth forever
Like a carrot I will be everything God can't see
Oh what do I mean
God can see everything
I mean the angels, I mean the half-gods
I mean the flowers, don't ever let them see me live forever
Don't you ever let them see
That I am all root here in the ground

**DORA
MALECH**

is the author of
Shore Ordered Ocean
(Waywiser, 2009)
and *Say So* (Cleve-
land State University
Poetry Center, 2010).
A graduate of Yale
University and the
Iowa Writers' Work-
shop, her poems have
appeared in *The New
Yorker, Poetry,* and *Best
New Poets,* among
other publications.
Distinguished Poet-
in-Residence at Saint
Mary's College of
California in 2011, she
has been the recipient
of honors that include
a Writers' Fellowship
at the Civitella Rani-
eri Center and a Ruth
Lilly Poetry Fellow-
ship. She coordinates
the Iowa Youth Writ-
ing Project, a lan-
guage arts outreach
program.

LOVE POEM

If by *truth* you mean *hand* then yes
I hold to be self-evident and hold you in the highest—
KO to my OT and bait to my switch, I crown
you one-trick pony to my one-horse town,
dub you my one-stop shopping, my space heater,
juke joint, tourist trap, my peep show, my meter reader,
you best batteries-not-included baring all or
nothing. Let me begin by saying *if he hollers,*
end with *goes the weasel.* In between,
cream filling. *Get over it,* meaning, *the moon.*
Tell me you'll dismember this night forever,
you my punch-drunking bag, tar to my feather.
More than the sum of our private parts, we are some
peekaboo, some peak and valley, some
bright equation (if *and* then *but,* if *er* then *uh*).
My fruit bat, my gewgaw. You had me at *no duh*.

LYING DOWN WITH DOGS

Fetch this phenomenominal conjesture. This time I mean it. A wag of the wand and the restive history sits like a sure thing. Suppositious (delicious) hypotheosis. Like lips could love a rubber teat. Miss *stay*, miss *beg*. Mistake the clock's tick-tock for some synecdochetic-tocking heart. No such touch as specious scratch of scruff or tummy. Name the litter after our best senses—Salty, Sweet, Sour, True and False. Lexiconic misprojections, *good* is *good* for ours and only, subspurious as in—if that's a puggle, my Grandpa's a cockapoo. Grandma's a labradoodle. Belly up's uncle and auntie's asleep at the top of the weaning pile. Paws is a cheap shot. Make it feel real like aposiopesis like—but never mind. This is *what army* sanitized for your protection. Mine match the alleles on the leash in question. Curled with the girls like a six-pack of commas. Got my licks in. Got my chihuzzahs. Sure I'm guilty. My dream date's to dig to China. Tongue to every spill and tail between. Haven't heard the last of Grandma. Ask any canny canine if it's rough. It's rough. I do it every chance I get.

COUNTRY SONGS

My man does his crying on a fast horse.
I do my best dancing with strangers.
The child screams through the moment
of silent prayer, says "It's a free country,"
says "You and what army." You can't
trespass on a river, you're only in
the wrong when you step out of it
into this field. All false hopes translate
to *just beginnings*. There was no grace
of God. I went. No secret that the sun and
moon have always slept in separate beds.
Gives some steel, steals some time and
calls it "borrowed," bruises and calls it
"something blue." A red bird, a yellow bird,
not in the same hour's frame but close
enough for their color together to make
a kind of ringing. I thought he brought
the water from the spring but he's still
bringing. I delegated. My job is waiting.
Is drinking water. I'm learning to say
"It's a free country: this army, but not me."

HUMILITY & CO.

I left a little cake, a little note:
I'm sorry if I threw up on your Christmas.
Dear, you can call it catharsis, it's still
bad manners. As if it were possible
to cancel all the flux inside, one wakes,
a levitating magnet. This is physics,
friends: the law of tell-you-when-you're-older,
ends that justify a good cry on
an iffy shoulder in the interregnum.
Wire-mother loves to cuddle the holidays
away, swings her dinner bell and waits
for drooling. Here, the crossroads of psychosis
and bad grammar where "someone" becomes "they"
and no one cares anymore. I guess I just
mean inexact, the loss or at the very
least a lack of basics. Take a penny,
leave a penny. It's been a pleasure. Close
the door gently and please hit the hall light
when you leave. One option is embrace
stasis, and yet some days the heart's
this dirty, matted mutt trembling at the feet
of the family passing time between trains
in the station café: "Look, Mom! It wants
something!" Let's walk down and watch them
fire the cannon. Let's see if they're still putting
the puppet show on in this rain.

14: What's your favorite sport?

Bar Trivia
Baseball x4
Basketball x9
Biking
Catch
Chess
Commuter Bicycling
Competitive Eating
Cribbage
Cricket
Diving
Fly Fishing
Football
Four Square
Hockey
Mini-golf
Newcomb
Olympic Swimming
Poetry
Rugby
Running
Sex
Skateboarding
Soccer
Solitaire
Surfing
Swimming
Video Games
Waking the Dead
Wit

SARAH MANGUSO is the author of the memoirs *The Guardians* (2012) and *The Two Kinds of Decay* (2008), the story collection *Hard to Admit and Harder to Escape* (2007), and the poetry collections *Siste Viator* (2006) and *The Captain Lands in Paradise* (2002). Honors for her writing include a Hodder Fellowship and the Rome Prize. She lives in Brooklyn.

THE RIDER

Some believe the end will come in the form of a mathematical equation.
Others believe it will descend as a shining horse.
I calculate the probabilities to be even at fifty percent:
Either a thing will happen or it won't.
I open a window,
I unmake the bed,
Somehow, I am moving closer to the equation or to the horse with everything I do.
Death comes in the form of a horse covered in shining equations.
There will be no further clues, I see.
I begin to read my horse.
The equations are drawn in the shapes of horses:
Horses covered in equations.
I am tempted to hook an ankle around the world as I ride away.
For I am about to ride far beyond the low prairie of beginnings and endings.

WILD GOOSE CHASE

My desperation was like that—
I was clambering up a fire escape on Houston Street
in hot pursuit while there it was,
lying on a beach in Oregon.
If I could only perceive it, see how large it was,
and be persuaded of its finitude.
You share a detail and I share a detail
and there we are, boring one another
with such sad banalities as we deserve.
I thought I recalled my adversary
playing chemin-de-fer on B Deck
but it was only me, sitting in a red dress,
imbibing red drinks. I can't
always recognize myself. Who's there?
or there? Pluck the tune on a zither,
carve the words on a stone slab. Make something,
anything. My desperation called to me, murmuring,
I leaned in to kiss it, and it was gone.
The source of it, deep in some distant volcano,
had to be quenched. I was all set
to go on an important journey, to buy
the phrasebook and read it on the boat, getting ready
for the cool wind across my face, fires burning in the sky
and the geese of mourning crossing overhead
as if in a daze and as if themselves an indication of hope.

WHAT CONCERNS ME NOW

What concerns me now is already done.
Predictions are wasted on me.

What concerns me now is waking up ecstatically
As when the cat meows the whole day and then grows quiet
Or the king takes off his crown and rolls it down the hill.

Physicists write of two possible fates of the universe,
Each dependent on a hypothetical amount of dark matter.
The two amounts are described as *a small amount* and *a large amount*.

The more complicated things become,
The simpler they are to understand
When explained by someone who already understands them.

What isn't like this?

What concerns me now is this drag queen shouting her monologue into the sky
Which is not so much there as it is visible to the tourists that walk under it.

Who can say when *act* becomes *light*?

The sun, a rictus in that sky—
Encoded with the outer limit of life on Earth, the ultimate death's head.

What concerns me now is this need to stop lying.
The so-called pain that fills my heart is actually located elsewhere.
As for the heart, it's nothing but empty space
And all it ever fills with is my own blood.

What concerns me now is this large animal swimming lovingly toward me.

HELL

The second-hardest thing I have to do is not be longing's slave.

Hell is that. Hell is that, others, having a job, and not having a job. Hell is thinking continually of those who were truly great.

Hell is the moment you realize you were ignorant of the fact, when it was true, that you were not yet ruined by desire.

The kind of music I want to continue hearing after I'm dead is the kind that makes me think I'll be capable of hearing it then.

There is music in Hell. Wind of desolation! It blows past the egg-eyed statues. The canopic jars are full of secrets.

The wind blows through me. I open my mouth to speak.

I recite the list of people I have copulated with. It does not take long. I say the names of my imaginary children. I call out four-syllable words beginning with B. This is how I stay alive.

Beelzebub. Brachiosaur. Bubble-headed. I don't know how I stay alive. What I do know is that there is a light, far above us, that goes out when we die,

and that in Hell there is a gray tulip that grows without any sun. It reminds me of everything I failed at,

and I water it carefully. It is all I have to remind me of you.

15: What is the last book of poetry you read?

A Larger Country, Tomás Q. Morin

Appetite, Aaron Smith

Balloon Pop Outlaw Black,
Patricia Lockwood

Dear Pierre, Karen Weiser

Debts & Lessons, Lynn Xu

Either Way I'm Celebrating,
Sommer Browning

Family System, Jack Christian

Fort Red Border, Kiki Petrosino

God's Silence, Franz Wright

Gust, Greg Alan Brownderville

Imaginary Logic, Rodney Jones

leadbelly, Tyehimba Jess

Lid to the Shadow, Alexandria Peary

Love, Death, and the Changing of the
Seasons, Marilyn Hacker

Manhater, Danielle Pafunda

Meme, Susan Wheeler

Music for Porn, Rob Halpern

Must a Violence, Oni Buchanan

Negro League Baseball, Harmony Holiday

North, Seamus Heaney

Palm Trees, Nick Twemlow

Paradise, Indiana, Bruce Snider

People Who Like Meatballs, Selima Hill

Pilfer, Andy Carter

Pink Reef, Robert Fernandez

Revolutionary Letters, Diane di Prima

Star in the Eye, James Shea

Strike Anywhere, Dean Young

Tender Hooks, Beth Ann Fennelly

The Dead Alive and Busy, Alan Shapiro

The /n/oulipian Analects, ed. Matias
Viegener and Christine Wertheim

The Chameleon Couch,
Yusef Komunyakaa

The Crisis of Infinite Worlds, Dana Ward

The Dollmaker's Ghost, Larry Levis

The French Exit, Elisa Gabbert

The Late Parade, Adam Fitzgerald

the new black, Evie Shockley

The Poems of Emily Dickinson, Emily
Dickinson, (ed. R.W. Franklin)

The Rings of Saturn, W.G. Sebald

The Transfer Tree, Karena Youtz

Work from Memory, Dan Beachy-Quick
and Matthew Goulish

RANDALL MANN

was born in Provo, Utah, in 1972, and grew up mainly in Kentucky and Florida. He was educated at the University of Florida. Mann is the author of three collections of poetry, *Straight Razor* (Persea Books, 2013), *Breakfast with Thom Gunn* (University of Chicago, 2009), shortlisted for the Lambda Literary Award and California Book Award, and *Complaint in the Garden* (Zoo Press, 2004), winner of the Kenyon Review Prize. His poems and prose have appeared in *The Washington Post, The Paris Review, The New Republic, Poetry,* and *Kenyon Review.* He lives in San Francisco.

POEM BEGINNING WITH A LINE BY JOHN ASHBERY

Jealousy. Whispered weather reports.
The lure of the land so strong it prompts
gossip: we chatter like small birds
at the edge of the ocean gray, foaming.

Now sand under sand hides
the buried world, the one in which our fathers failed,
the palm frond a dangerous truth
they once believed, and touched. Bloodied their hands.

They once believed. And, touched, bloodied their hands;
the palm frond, a dangerous truth;
the buried world, the one in which our fathers failed.
Now sand under sand hides

at the edge of the ocean: gray, foaming
gossip. We chatter like small birds,
the lure of the land so strong it prompts
jealousy. Whispered weather reports.

THE MORTICIAN IN SAN FRANCISCO

This may sound queer,
but in 1985 I held the delicate hands
of Dan White:
I prepared him for burial; by then, Harvey Milk
was made monument—no, myth—by the years
since he was shot.

I remember when Harvey was shot:
twenty, and I knew I was queer.
Those were the years,
Levi's and leather jackets holding hands
on Castro Street, cheering for Harvey Milk—
elected on the same day as Dan White.

I often wonder about Supervisor White,
who fatally shot
Mayor Moscone and Supervisor Milk,
who was one of us, a Castro queer.
May 21, 1979: a jury hands
down the sentence, seven years—

in truth, five years—
for ex-cop, ex-fireman Dan White,
for the blood on his hands;
when he confessed that he had shot
the mayor and the queer,
a few men in blue cheered. And Harvey Milk?

Why cry over spilled milk,
some wondered, semi-privately, for years—
it meant "one less queer."
The jurors turned to White.
If just the mayor had been shot,
Dan might have had trouble on his hands—

but the twelve who held his life in their hands
maybe didn't mind the death of Harvey Milk;
maybe, the second murder offered him a shot
at serving only a few years.
In the end, he committed suicide, this Dan White.
And he was made presentable by a queer.

THE FALL OF 1992

Gainesville, Florida

An empire of moss,
   dead yellow, and carapace:
that was the season
   of gnats, amyl nitrate, and goddamn
rain; of the gator in the fake lake rolling

his silverish eyes;
   of vice; of *Erotica,*
give it up and let
   me have my way. And the gin-soaked dread
that an acronym was festering inside.

Love was a doorknob
   statement, a breakneck goodbye—
and the walk of shame
   without shame, the hair disheveled, curl
of Kools, and desolate birds like ampersands...

I re-did my face
   in the bar bathroom, above
the urinal trough.
   I liked it rough. From behind the stall,
Lady Pearl slurred the words: *Don't hold out for love.*

STRAIGHT RAZOR

He slid the stiff blade up to my ear:
Oh, fear,

this should have been thirst, a cheapening act.
But I lacked,

as usual, the crucial disbelief. Sticky, cold,
a billfold

wet in my mouth, wrists bound by his belt,
I felt

like the boy in a briny night pool, he who found
the drowned

body, yet still somehow swam with an unknown joy.
That boy.

SABRINA ORAH MARK
is the author
of two books of
prose poems,
The Babies (Sat-
urnalia Books,
2004) and *Tsim
Tsum* (Satur-
nalia Books,
2009), as well
as the chap-
book *Walter B.'s
Extraordinary
Cousin Arrives
for a Visit & Oth-
er Tales* (Wood-
land Editions,
2006). She has
received fellow-
ships from the
Fine Arts Work
Center in Prov-
incetown and
the National
Endowment for
the Arts.

THE VERY NERVOUS FAMILY

Mr. Horowitz clutches a bag of dried apricots to his chest. Although the sun is shining, there will probably be a storm. Electricity will be lost. Possibly forever. When this happens the very nervous family will be the last to starve. Because of the apricots. "Unless," says Mrs. Horowitz, "the authorities confiscate the apricots." Mr. Horowitz clutches the bag of dried apricots tighter. He should've bought two bags. One for the authorities and one for his very nervous family. Mrs. Horowitz would dead bolt the front door to keep the authorities out, but it is already bolted. Already dead. She doesn't like that phrase. Dead bolt. It reminds her of getting shot before you even have a chance to run. "Everyone should have at least a *chance* to run," says Mrs. Horowitz. "Don't you agree, Mr. Horowitz?" Mrs. Horowitz always refers to her husband as Mr. Horowitz should they ever one day become strangers to each other. Mr. Horowitz agrees. When the authorities come they should give the Horowitzs a chance to run before they shoot them for the apricots. Eli Horowitz, their very nervous son, rushes in with his knitting. "Do not rush," says Mr. Horowitz, "you will fall and you will die." Eli wants ice skates for his birthday. "We are not a family who ice skates!" shouts Mrs. Horowitz. She is not angry. She is a mother who simply does not wish to outlive her only son. Mrs. Horowitz gathers her very nervous son up in her arms, and gently explains that families who ice skate become the ice they slip on. The cracks they fall through. The frost that bites them. "We have survived this long to become our own demise?" asks Mrs. Horowitz. "No," whispers Eli, "we have not." Mr. Horowitz removes one dried apricot from the bag and nervously begins to pet it when Mrs. Horowitz suddenly gasps. She thinks she may have forgotten to buy milk. Without milk they will choke on the apricots. Eli rushes to the freezer with his knitting. There is milk. The whole freezer is stuffed with milk. Eli removes a frozen half pint and glides it across the kitchen table. It is like the milk is skating. He wishes he were milk. Brave milk. He throws the half pint on the floor and stomps on it. Now the milk is crushed. Now the milk is dead. Now the Horowitzs are that much closer to choking. Mr. and Mrs. Horowitz are dumbfounded. Their very nervous son might be a maniac. He is eight. God is punishing them for being survivors. God has given them a maniac for a son. All they ask is that they not starve, and now their only son is killing milk. Who will marry their maniac? No one. Who will mother their grandchildren? There will be no grandchildren. All they ask is that there is something left of them when they are shot for the apricots, but now their only son is a maniac who will give them no grandchildren. Mr. Horowitz considers leaving Eli behind when he and Mrs. Horowitz run for their lives.

WHERE BABIES COME FROM

"Where," asked Beatrice, "do babies come from?" Walter B. was hanging a painting in the crawl space. It was a painting of the babies. "Basically," said Walter B., "babies come from rubbing babies together. They rub and they rub. Once, I heard them rubbing." "Are you sure those are the babies where babies come from?" asked Beatrice. She was staring at the painting. It was a painting of the babies. Walter B. stepped back. "They seem," said Beatrice, "to be different babies." Walter B. tilted his head. A door slammed. They stood for a long time and examined the painting. Beatrice was right. These were not the same babies. These were different babies. Some of these babies carried twine. These were not the babies where babies came from. Some of these babies were not rubbing. Some of these babies had books about babies tucked under their arms. These were not the same babies. These babies would never be the babies where babies came from. These babies were different. And Beatrice was the first to call their bluff.

THE BABIES

Some thought it was because of all the babies I suddenly seemed to be having. Others, that I should pay for the damages. Fact is, I wasn't getting any older so I bought a small aquarium, and skipped town. Took up with a toy store owner until he left me for a more beautiful robot. Took up with a reader of instructional booklets. Never mind. I was lost. By the time I arrived at Mrs. Greenaway's, it was clear I was nowhere at all. In exchange for room and board, I'd rearrange her furniture, her birthmarks, her quiet animals, until they took on more satisfying shapes. Sometimes the shapes were simple, like a mustache or a pipe. Sometimes they were more complicated arrangements, like the one of dead Mr. Greenaway's closed barbershop. Over the years, as Mrs. Greenaway and I became more and more vague, the shapes did too. For identification purposes, we'd give them names like *She Wasn't Fooling Anyone, She Was Hurt And She Was Hurt Bad* or *The Insides of Doctors.* One night when I was working on a piece I thought I'd call *Symphony, Symphony* the shapes began to slip out of my hands. At first, as Mrs. Greenaway remembers, the sound of broken glass. Then the trumpets. Then the terrible music of all those babies I once seemed to be suddenly having, marching, like soldiers, in rows. Then their round wet bellies coming towards me. Mrs. Greenaway still talks about how expertly they gathered me into their tiny arms. And how they took me away not like a prisoner. But like a mother. Into a past I still swear I never had.

16: What is your mother's first name?

A very southern name that reminds
me of ocean and Arkansas

Ann x2

Annette

Barbara

Betsy x2

Carole

Cheryl

Cindy

Cynthia

Deborah

Dona

Eiko

Emily

Gem of the Ocean

Jackie

Jere

Jo

Judith

Judy

Kari (or Karl)

Kathryn

Kathy

Linda

Lois

Mary x2

Maureen

Neomia

Patricia x2

Renée

Rita

Robyn

Rose

Socorro

Susan

Valerie

CHRIS MARTIN

is the author of *American Music* (Copper Canyon, 2007) and *Becoming Weather* (Coffee House Press, 2011). He is also the author of several chapbooks, including *How to Write a Mistake-ist Poem* (Brave Men, 2011), *enough* (Ugly Duckling, 2012), and the serially released *CHAT* (Flying Object, 2012). He is an editor at Futurepoem books and lives in Minneapolis with his wife, the poet Mary Austin Speaker.

JOKES FOR STRANGERS

All twenty-first-century
Day long I compose these jokes
For myself and strangers

For the cats also, stuck
As they are in the airshaft
As am I, breath

Meandering through its conspiratorial
Orbits, circling the eyes
Which goggle sprightly, peering

Into the habitual arrangements and I
Am a joke too sometimes
The way a horse burns down

To bridle and the mind lingers
On cake, we are all plastic
Miniatures trembling amidst the acoustics

Electrified, my sword bending like
A cactus, the ruthless wind
Upon it, I thought it terribly

Important to bed
A woman of learning
To feel *The Sonnets*

And fill the empty drawer
A bus stampedes
Down Ninth Street, cauterizing

Certain possibilities of space
I can't tell you
How much it means to lose even

An unwanted quantity
Of variousness, as perhaps
All my decisions end

With hard looks into the oily distance
Of urban mirage, fuck
Not getting a job, I've got kids

To learn, Palestinian
Kids, Italian kids, kids like myself wrung
Whiter each genealogical turn and

Who's looking out for us? The president? Even
Cars crossing the street are doomed
To simple sympathizing over the inglorious

Physics of contact, they are not human
And therefore have no problem
Staving off the delirium of hate, you have not

Died before, you are no
Perverted ghost lifting a skirt
With the empty pang

Of regret, you are not the resurrection of George
De Chirico, who died the year Denver
Lost its first Super Bowl, the year I was

Weaned and stamps cost an unlucky
Thirteen cents, which doesn't mean colonnades
Are any less haunted, mustachioed women

Rolling tremendous wheels of cheese
Along their claustrophobic geometries
I may have lost

My attention for Logic
But I see beautiful
Children circumventing cruelty

Nearly every day and it begs
The question—what have you done
Lately for the safety

Of our feelings? Have you
Offered your seat on a crowded
Downtown subway car

To a man in perfect physical health
Because he had tears in his eyes? Neither
Have I, not yet, but at least

I considered it in writing.

TRAJECTORY OF A THIEF

It's simple, a life
Of eccentric guessing
You move

To California, one drunk
Night you climb
Every fence in the neighborhood

And no one shoots you
And fog washes
The church steeple

Bare, months
Pass, you sell your car
To a surfer, move

Again, America roils, a man
Walks into a bar and then drives
Into a tree, you move

Again, one love
Recedes and another beckons
Brightly, your roommate

Gets rich and it befits
Her, the sun
Struggles over your eastward

Facing sill and it never
Occurs to you
To wonder how

It's happening, it's simple
Yves Klein invents
A color and it kills him

You steal six hundred thousand
Hours from god and fear
Capture constantly, one wriggling

Dactyl amidst the day's lapidary
Scansion, you carry on
Unreasonably and bloodless

The moon is a rock that salutes
You for it, you forgo
Certain dignities, others

Are thrust upon you, animals
Curve to your touch, a Brooklyn boy
With an unpronounceable name

Writes *Fire is tasty*
You imbecile, the leaves
In the trees in

The park ignite and you climb
The fire escape to the roof
To chart the buildings' unwavering

Ballet of windows, bullets
Are cocked nearby, the cops drink
Beer from Styrofoam

Cups on the street below
Ted takes you to Chinatown for turtle
Soup, each piece

Of its floating meat
Wholly disparate, the cherry
Blossoms arrive and then

Dissipate triumphantly
Like the sting
Of winter, cephalopods slowly

Adapt, an anonymous
Russian woman saves you
From falling on

The subway, the rooftop
Reads GODOT, the waitress
At the diner calls

You Professor, it's simple
The wind hits
Your lips and you're

Pleased, a deer hits
Your father's car and you're
Inconsolable, a family

Of skunks makes purchase
Beneath the floorboards
And the impending decision puzzles

You—the stink or
The killing it
Takes to rid yourself

Of it, of them, who else?

J. MICHAEL MARTINEZ lives in Denver and is pursuing a PhD at the University of Colorado Boulder. His first book received the Academy of American Poets' Walt Whitman Award.

from *ICONOLOGIA:*

or a Selection of Chrestomathies
regarding a Human Singularity

Imagine—in front of us—they silently pass. And they believe unrelated
        objects are machines
for recognizing the human. And, again, we are no longer interruptions.

Imagine—in front of us—the beginning is not a study. And they believe
        the cicada's larva
reveals narrow secrets. And we accompany: to form, to shape.

Imagine—in front of us—a beautiful garden. And they believe color is the
        shoreline's end
where we abandon our too sudden bodies. And, here, we are carriers
        of different significance.

Imagine—in front of us—each word devolves a lexicon. And they believe
        shape shuts on a hinge
within the voice they fable. And, here, we slaughter the spring lambs.

Imagine—in front of us—they pass us between nature, between history.
        And they believe the door
frame alters the curtains' flow. And we are a dark summer moving against
        oceans.

Imagine starlings circling in a postcard's blue. And they believe oration is
        the living thing, the end
of geometric space. And here, in full sunlight, we are gifts hoisted
        to the vanishing point.

Cultural theorist Justin Read writes in *Modern Poetics & Hemispheric American Cultural Studies,* "The 'American' comes into being as a result of migration & encounter . . . there is no such thing as 'American' until two extant cultures meet & are thereby compelled to communicate, even if this results in miscommunication" (xxii). The concept of an "American" emerges only in modern historical discourse after the conquest—in the betweenness of two extant cultures; the American, in other words, is a body of migration & encounter. If the American only emerges in liminal dialogue, the American language itself is a migratory act; as Read correctly asserts, there is no American language per se: the languages of the Americas are divided—English, Spanish, French—have origin in Europe; the native languages of indigenous peoples find their voices pre-Conquest. If one can name an "American" language, it is the translation & migration of meaning (lost) in the encounter between discourses.

we other hunger   *the flower whose roots succor*

the changless

intimacies

the un *of communion*   *shaped from deeper root*

SELF-PORTRAIT AS YOUR VOICE, TRYING TO STOP AN ECHO

wherever tidal water

      foams salt-
      water flowers

      against stone

      darker we echo

wed to a death

      grown young
      our tears

      learn of radiance

outside gravity   we will say we are

      angels in the children
      our bodies were

      such species wholly present tense

/ˈædəm/

[Hebrew *a-dām* mān, earth.]

i. The name given in the Bible to the first man; hence *fig.* as in the phrase *Old Adam*, the 'old man' of St. Paul (*Rom.* vi. 6, etc.): the unregenerate condition or character.

ii. Phr. *not to know* (a person) *from Adam*: not to recognize him; *(as) old as Adam*: primevally old.

—OED

I   unwrapped   the   light   from   origin's
aviary,   wing & brittle beak
sewed   through an apron of
leaves. I pinned her pining   against a brittle
hymn. I bit her lip to pulse   our organ
& thresh desire for salt.   For the
heart's other hunger, the skin in wondrous agony,
I said, he gazed the sound.   I
meant she split the plot. He said, I, I said
her   letters fell
from my dress of flesh,   every edge
an erosion unsheathed from speech.

17: What's the name of your favorite teacher of all time?

All of them

Aurora Camacho de Schmidt

Beau Valtz

Beverly

Caryl

Cora Five

Dean Young

Doc Bee

Emily Taylor

Eve Hunnings

Friends

George Kalamaras

Hubert McAlexander

Jayne Hanlin

John Gery

Kenneth Koch

Laura Mullen

Levine

Max Jacob

Mom

Mr. Dickerson

Mr. Edwards

Mr. Morwick

Mr. William Sequin

Mrs. Barksdale aka Granny B.

Ms. Allen

Ms. Curran

Ms. Tegenfeldt

Norman Dubie

Patricia

Peter Sacks

Philip Levine

Sterling Plumpp

Steve Orlen

The Swedish Chef

Tom Walsh

Too many to name

Walter Bartman

William Logan

William Prottengeier

ADRIAN MATEJKA

is the author of *The Devil's Garden* (Alice James Books, 2003) and *Mixology* (Penguin, 2009), which was a winner of the 2008 National Poetry Series. His new collection, *The Big Smoke*, was published by Penguin in 2013. He is the recipient of two Illinois Arts Council Literary Awards and fellowships from Cave Canem and the Lannan Foundation. His work has appeared or is forthcoming in *American Poetry Review, Best American Poetry 2010, Ploughshares,* and *Poetry* among other journals and anthologies. He teaches at Indiana University in Bloomington.

ENGLISH B

I had to be introduced to The Man.
He was around before 1977.
I just couldn't see him, like air
or welfare. My mom told me:
No matter what you do, the man
is going to try and keep you down.
I already knew no one was keeping
me down. So when teacher asked
me to read from Kaleidoscopes,
I told her *back off, white woman.*
I'm not reading your books.
She laughed, but understood
when I threw my book, covers
flapping like man's first scraps
with gravity. Teacher realized
she wasn't keeping me down,
so I got sent to Remedial English.
When I looked up "remedial,"
the dictionary read: "The Man
questioning your authenticity."
Then I looked up "authenticity."
Dictionary definition: "Blackness."
So I was authentic and the Man
could keep his remedial. Problems
began when I realized my mom
was The Man, too: five feet
two inches, a little heavy with curling
red afro, white with power fist
in the air. Then, a half-black, half-
white boy sitting on the stoop,
counting pieces of glass,
trying not to keep himself down.

BATTLE ROYAL

Jack Johnson

Back then, they'd chain a bear
in the middle of the bear garden

& let the dogs loose. Iron chains
around a bear's neck don't slow

him too much. A bear will always
make short work of a dog. Shakespeare

said Sackerson did it more than
twenty times to dogs & wildcats

alike. & since most creatures
are naturally afraid of bears, there

wouldn't always be much of a show
in the bear garden. So the handlers

sometimes put the bear's eyes out
or took his teeth to make the fight

more sporting. I believe you need
eyes more than you need teeth

in a fight, but losing either makes
a bear a little less mean. Once baiting

was against the law, some smart
somebody figured coloreds fight

just as hard if hungry enough.
So they rounded up the skinniest

of us, had us strip to trousers, then
blindfolded us before the fight.

They turned us in hard circles a few
times on the ring steps like a motorcar

engine before pushing us between
the ropes. When the bell rang,

it seemed like I got hit from eight
directions. I didn't know where

those punches came from, but I swung
so hard my shoulder hasn't been right

since because the man said only
the last darky on his feet gets a meal.

GOLD SMILE

Jack Johnson

> *Teeth hadst thou in thy head when thou wast born,*
> *To signify thou camest to bite the world:*
> —Henry VI

They call teeth *dent* in France & the name
makes sense the way teeth do what they do
to bacon & shoulders & cakes. The French
word for gold is *or*, so when the folks in Paris

describe my smile it sounds like what
happens when I punch a door: *dents d'or*.
Dents d'or, the French children say when
I open wide. *Dents d'or*, Etta says when she

locks herself in the powder room. Tommy
Burns said *dents d'or* when I was hooking him
into asking for forgiveness. His people back
in Canada would have said the same thing

if they were in Sydney to witness our spectacle.
Before we got into the ring, I told Tommy
the only reason I got gold uppers was to make
every bite of my food twice as expensive.

UNFUNKY UFO, 1981

The first Space Shuttle launch got delayed until Sunday,
so we watched the shuttle's return in class instead—
PS 113's paunchy black & white rolled in, its antennae
adjusted sideways & down for better reception so the set
looked like a teenager after his love letter got returned
to sender. The same day, Garrett jacked my new pencil
box. The same day, Cynthia peed her jeans instead of going
to the bathroom & letting Garrett jack her pencil box.
Both of us, too upset to answer questions about space
flight, so we got sent to the back of the class. Me, smelling
like the kind of shame that starts bar fights on Tuesday
afternoons. She smelled like pee & denim. The shuttle
made its slick way back to Earth, peeling clouds from
the monochromatic sky & we all—even the back of the bus
& astronomically marginal—were winners. American,
because a few days before, a failed songwriter put a bullet
in the President in the name of Jodie Foster after she
returned his love songs unopened. The shuttle looked
like a bullet, only with wings & a cockpit, & when it landed,
the class broke into applause & the teacher snatched
a thinning American flag from the corner, waved it back
& forth in honor of the President & those astronauts.

**JOHN
MURILLO'S**

first poetry collection, *Up Jump
the Boogie* (Cypher, 2010), was
a finalist for both the 2011 Kate
Tufts Discovery Award and the
PEN Open Book Award, and was
named by *Huffington Post* as one
of "Ten Recent Books of Poetry
You Should Read Right Now." A
graduate of New York University's
MFA program in creative writing,
his other honors include a Pushcart
Prize, two Larry Neal Writers
Awards, and fellowships from the
Bread Loaf Writers Conference,
Cave Canem Foundation, the Fine
Arts Work Center in Provincetown,
The New York Times, and the
Wisconsin Institute of Creative
Writing. His work has appeared in
such publications as *Callaloo, Court
Green, Ninth Letter, Ploughshares*,
and *Angles of Ascent: A Norton
Anthology of African-American Poetry.*
A founding member of the poetry
collective The Symphony, he has
taught at Cornell University,
New York University, Columbia
College Chicago, and the University
of Wisconsin–Madison.

ENTER THE DRAGON

—Los Angeles, California, 1976

For me, the movie starts with a black man,
Leaping into an orbit of badges, tiny moons

Catching the sheen of his perfect black afro.
Arc kicks, karate chops, and thirty cops

On their backs. It starts with the swagger,
The cool lean into the leather front seat

Of the black and white he takes off in,
Deep hallelujahs of moviegoers drowning

Out the *wah wah* guitar, salt & butter
High-fives, *Right on, brother*! and Daddy

Glowing so bright he can light the screen
All by himself. This is how it goes down.

Friday night and my father drives us
Home from the late show, two heroes

Cadillacking across King Boulevard.
In the car's dark cab, we jab and clutch,

Jim Kelly and Bruce Lee with popcorn
Breath, and almost miss the lights flashing

In the cracked side mirror. I know what's
Under the seat, but when the uniforms

Approach from the rear quarter panel,
When the fat one leans so far into my father's

Window I can smell his long day's work,
When my father—this John Henry of a man—

Hides his hammer, doesn't buck, tucks away
His baritone, license and registration shaking as if

Showing a bathroom pass to a grade school
Principal, I learn the difference between cinema

And city, between the moviehouse cheers
Of old men and the silence that gets us home.

PRACTICING FADE-AWAYS

—after Larry Levis

On a deserted playground in late day sun,
My palms dusted black, dribbling
A worn, leather ball behind my back, this loneliness
Echoes from the handball courts nearby.
Nearly all the markings—free throw lane, sideline,
Center circle—rubbed to nothing.
A crack in the earth cuts across the schoolyard,
Jagged as a scar on a choir boy's cheek.

Twenty years ago,
I ran this very court with nine other
Wanna-be ballers. We'd steal
Through peeled chain links, or hop
The gate to get here: our blacktop Eden.
One boy, who had a funny pigeon-toed set shot
And a voice full of church bells, sang spirituals
Every time he made a basket,
The other boys humming along, laughing,
High-fives flying down the court.

And a boy we called 'The Sandman'
For how he put you to sleep with his shoulder fake or drop step.
Over six feet tall in the tenth grade,
Smooth talker with an itch for older guys' girlfriends.
One Sunday morning, they found him stabbed to death
Outside the Motel 6, pockets untouched,
Bills folded neatly against his beautiful cooling thigh.
And 'Downtown' Ricky Brown,
Whose family headed west when he was two,
But still called himself a New Yorker,
Who never pulled from less than thirty feet out
And could bank shots blindfolded.

He went to Grambling, drove himself
Crazy with conspiracy theories and liquor,
Was last seen roaming the French Quarter, shoeless, babbling
About the Illuminati's six-hundred sixty-six ways
To enslave the populace.

At sixteen, I discovered
Venice Beach, with its thousand bodybuilders,
Roller skates, and red thong bikinis.
I would stand on the sidelines and watch
The local ballplayers, leaping and hollering
Quicksilver giants, run and gun,
Already grown into their man bodies,
Funkadelic rising from a boombox in the sand.
Now, all I hear are chain nets chiming as I sink
One fade-away after another,
The backboard, the pole, throwing a long shadow
Across the cracked black asphalt.

What the nets want must be this caress,
This stillness stretching
Along every avenue, over high school
Gymnasiums and deserted playgrounds,
And the ambulance drivers drifting into naps
Back at the station house.
What the boys who ran these courts wanted was
A lob pass high enough
To pull them into the sky,
Something they could catch in both hands
And hang from,
Long enough for someone to snap
A photograph, to hold them there,
Skybound. Risen.

SONG

I know it's wrong to stare, but it's Tuesday,
The express is going local, and this woman's

Thighs—cocoa-buttered, crossed, and stacked
To her chin—are the only beauty I think I'll see

for the next forty minutes. Not the train's
Muttering junkie, who pauses a little too long

In front of me, dozing, but never losing balance.
Not the rat we notice scurry past the closing doors,

Terrorizing the rush hour platform. Not
Even these five old Black men, harmonizing

About begging and pride, about a woman
Who won't come home. But skin, refracted

Light, and the hem's hard mysteries. I imagine
There's a man somewhere in this city, working

Up the nerve to beg this woman home, the sweet
Reconciliation of sweat on sweat, and pride

Not even afterthought. My own woman, who
I've begged sometimes not to leave, and begged

Sometimes please to leave, never has, also waits,
Uptown, in a fourth floor walk-up, in an old t-shirt

For me to make it back. She waits for me to come
Through jungles, over rivers, out from underground.

She waits, without fear, knowing no matter what,
I will make it home. And, God, there were times

I probably shouldn't have, but did. And lived
To see this day, the junkies, rats, and thighs,

And I say, praise it all. Even this ride, its every
Bump and stall, and each funky body pressed

To another, sweat earned over hours, bent over moats,
Caged in cubicles, and after it all, the pouring

Of us, like scotch, into daylight. Dusk.
Rush hour. This long trip home. Praise it all.

The dead miss out on summer. The sun
Bouncing off moving trains and a woman

To love you when you get inside. Somewhere
In this city, a man will plead for love gone,

Another chance, and think himself miserable.
He'll know, somewhere deep, he may never

Win her back. But he'll know even deeper,
That there is a kind of joy in the begging

Itself, that all songs are love songs. Blues,
Especially. Praise the knowledge. Praise

The opening and closing doors, the ascent
Into light, heat, each sidewalk square, cracks

And all, the hundred and twelve stairs between
Lobby and my woman's front door, the exact

Moment I let in this city, let out this sweat,
And come to own this mighty, mighty joy.

THE NEW PREDICAMENT

states that no one is exempt. If you wake up on one side, you must. If you wake up on the other, again, there is no one to trust but. If you wake up and roll over, bump into a woman, all the more so. There is no bribe large enough, no drink strong enough to overcome the waves of people who will be waiting outside when you open your second-story balcony window. They may cheer, but more likely they will throw corn. Oh, they will throw corn. You will turn to your wife if you have one. She will rub her eyes. She will not say a thing, but the corn will come flying through the window. You will try hard not to look embarrassed. It will fly in silently.

What if she is hit by an ear?

LANGUAGE BARRIER

Men in America have a dog. I come back from Europe
and you have a dog but not. Men in Europe have. I bark
up the stairs and tap the tree for advice. Who has a dog.
Men with dogs more likely or less fetching or slightly
scarce as men without. When walking the dog, is all
about the stride. I can close my eyes and walk for a
long time without stepping on any dogshit. I must be
in America, so I open my eyes to watch out for men
instead. If I have ancient dogcrap on my shoe, I am in
France and have been. The men watch, and the women
have dogs. From the tree no one is shitting but is
conducive to watching. I am not concerned about birds
because they do not live on the ground and they barely
have feet. I am concerned with the placement of my
step after stepping down into soft or hard and your
voice is dry. A shy dry or a bored dry or a fake, dry but
really shy voice is not talking to me, thus the dog. No
dog speaks in this poem, nor do I have a dog, nor am I
speaking. Yet American men with dogs have. Although
there may still be some French dogpoo on my shoe, I
go over and talk. Talking to a dog is acceptable in any
language, thus the men. After that, it is not my problem
and you understand it as. You are American or European.
One dog gets drunk and this is a college town. One dog
has sex with a non-dog and this is pornography. One
dog shoots some shit and this is a Western. I go for a
walk and this is still in English and I am not interested
in dogs but men.

9.2.2003

Nightmare about hamburgers,

Having fallen into one.

Or rather, being swallowed by an avalanche of undercooked hamburger meat, I am in the pinkest part of it and try the spitting method to find out which way is up. I decide, however, that any direction is good enough so long as it is fast, as my assumption is that no hamburger can possibly go on forever. I worm my clothes off so that I can move easier, and am reminded of Carolee Schneemann's *Meat Joy* from the 60s, though I am finding no joy in this. I struggle to get my clothes back on as I realize that the friction from the clothes is necessary to overcome the grease so that I can get out of this place.

I think I see a light in the distance.

Though it might very easily be a lump of fat.

But worse yet, clearer yet, I begin to smell smoke, a gas-fired barbeque. I call out, distressed and damselled to the hilt:

"Hamburger!"
"Hamburger!"
"Hamburger!"

For lack of a better way to describe the situation – and I am quoting some long-lost love poem, and so I am.

9.19.2004

Whenever I meet new people I want to touch them first and find out their texture.

I also do this in stores when I am shopping, so shopkeepers hate me. I turn to the person on my left and ask very gently if I can lick his or her eyeball. The food arrives and I place a slice of raw cow tongue in my mouth, because someone once told me that this is absolutely the sexiest food item in the world. Do you like kissing cows.

I get up to go to the restroom, but the person on my right, instead of moving out of the way, offers to me his or her arm, with a large gash from last week's motorcycle accident. There is an awkward moment, and then I sit back down so that I am more stable. I clean off my right hand before I touch, ease my finger inside and then further, some asshole at the other end of the table is making stupid sound effects, but in any case I am soon unaware of everything oh no everything at all, and if I were not myself at this moment I would probably have to avert my eyes, unable to watch as a certain virginity is lost, and then lost.

18: What was the name of your imaginary friend or first pet?

Alicia

Ben and Maple (newts)

Bootsie

Chancleta

Checkers (cat)

Chico

Chippy

Chutzpah (bunny)

Crusty and Flour

Cyril

Diane

Edith Piaf (hamster)

Eric

Henry

Iggy

Joe (imaginary friend who owned several gas stations)

Licorice

Lucinda Labchow Lasky

Lucy

Magee

Mike the Dog

Misti (kitten)

Mittens

Mr. Miyagi (beta fish)

Nero

Patches

Poppy

Rene (goldfish)

Rodney (goldfish)

Saber

Scarlett O'Hara Mann

Shadow the Cat

Sniffie (rat)

Soggy (fish)

Snowy

Tess

Tia

Tito (fly)

Tony

KATHLEEN OSSIP

is the author of *The Cold War*, which was named one of *Publishers Weekly*'s 100 best books of 2011; *The Search Engine*, which won the American Poetry Review/Honickman First Book Prize; and *Cinephrastics*, a chapbook of movie poems. Poems have appeared in *Best American Poetry, Paris Review, Boston Review, American Poetry Review, Washington Post, The Believer, Fence,* and *Poetry Review* (London). She teaches at The New School. She was a co-founder of LIT, and she's the poetry editor of *Women's Studies Quarterly*. She has received a fellowship from the New York Foundation for the Arts.

THE COLD WAR

We were born in a tangle.
We met like pioneers, in a heap of tranquil junk.

K. wakes up, thinks about the past, is sad.

Thimbleberries, black, thud out of the light.
A suck: grit of sugar in the milk.
Flat front lawn, weeping willow shorn of grove.
The oozing leaves of grass, stink of petunias,
a stain like a wound, Mars-red in a livid sky.

Reverie. Craze of nostalgia.
Any sentence would have to begin with God,
Easterish, dense, a closely-reasoned argument
stripped of all pomp and mysticism –

To find: grace in a mangled world.

Wit, language play, confession, observation:
Personally, I was in the market for a more personal brand of art.
Burping the rubbermaid box, mom lay in
the conflict, the dream, and the reasons they wouldn't fly.

K. wishes she could show you: no heart is pure.

It was not that there was no enemy.
It was that we would never come to blows.

We know this now but didn't then:

    Trembling under the desk,
      plastic under the table,
        cold drafts from the cellar,
      a frail little fame.

(Did we live with terror?
"Useless to go back. Had to be. Tell me all."
               —James Joyce)
But the open spaces were beautiful:
Blanket flapping on a clothesline, clouds,
squall/bluster, chary mist. *Hurry. Pretty.*
If my buoyancy was contrived,
still it bristled for me.

                             My grandmother peeled a
                             baggy-skinned tangerine, she
                             made cinnamon sticks for me.
                             My other annotated *Jane*
                             Eyre. Two brothers, a sister—
                             full of ozone. Having not the
                             passion of an artist—

K.'s honesty isn't complete.
K. is trying to get closer.

It was just another of those crisp blue days;
nothing encouraged an inner life.

God is a mnemonic. Art is someone's name.
Tina Orsini's phone number comes upon me
and I am whelpish and adrift.   And three cabbage butterflies.

        Remembrance, a gift: TV offered its blue comfort.
In those days, when you dialed the phone,
someone answered it. Abstraction was everywhere.
We refused to sacrifice sanity, a sacrifice itself.

Poorly integrated, history wells up. If you can, make the leap with me:

A mind too lively (too lovely) has a beauty but not the right kind of beauty or the
best kind of beauty. Old-fashioned talk: At what point does precision become a
flaw?

K. must get herself down to the river.
K. wants to say fuck memory but what good will it do!

An heirdom waited just for *me.*
The Mohawk was one of *many* rivers.
I was trembling, in fear of the words *Suddenly the Mideast...*
I *could,* if I tried, love continuities.

        Restlessness the only grace I know.

The doors of the prison, flung open. When I finally was freed, it was as if I had been re-born. Everything shone as never before. Colors were brighter, more vivid, and I felt such happiness and benevolence toward all things that I could not bear to hurt even an ant.

I believe almost everything now.

Thought is active. It imposes. It takes & molds & adds & projects. It believes in its own authority. It requires bright light but sheds none. It reduces. Thought does not accommodate change.

Understanding yields. It unrolls for truth to rest on for a time. It accepts. It hides itself, so it will see and hear more; it opens wide, then wider.

Craft is a synthesis: thought in the service of understanding. Think hard in order to open to understanding: that is craft.

K. was hungrily made.

K. is an American creation.

K. cannot recommend realism.

K. cannot recommend surrealism.

K. cannot recommend plain speech.

K. cannot recommend free association.

K. can recommend song:

> *The tug of the past.*
> *Don't let go so fast*
> *of what you're haunted by—*
> *It'll last till it lasts.*

           The former things   pass away

Craft will take us through this wood.

**KIKI
PETROSINO**
is an assistant
professor of
English at the
University of
Louisville and
co-editor of
Transom, an
independent
online jour-
nal. She has
authored two
poetry collec-
tions: *Fort Red
Border* (Sara-
bande, 2009)
and *Hymn
for the Black
Terrific* (Sara-
bande, 2013).

THIS WILL DARKEN THE CABIN

Halfway through my plate of tiger prawns
Redford returns from the cockpit tour.
Such a face he says. *Were you this soulful as a child?*
He tips my chin & slides my headset back.
I've been listening to the pilots marking weather
in their code talk. Right now we're at two-five-five
knots, heading straight into the soup above
Las Vegas. Our pilot has a clean, grey voice—
like creosote or silverware. He's just said *advise*.
He's just said *preparing*. Redford eases
into his seat, folding one knee
over the other. He rolls his double brandy
in a plastic snifter. The cuffs of his soft green shirt
are pushed into his elbows. *I had some soulful ways, I guess.*
I tuck into a small ramekin of green gage plums
soaked in cream & rice vinegar. At the edge
of my vision, Redford lifts his spoon, considering
the loose pyramid of Asian jungle fowl
on his tray. I pick up a tiny package
of salt. *Know what I used to do with this?*
I reach across Redford's lap, taking a lengthy swallow
of brandy from his glass. *At night, I'd eat this.*
It was a thing. I'd pour a whole bunch
in my mouth, & then I'd chew until my tongue opened.
For the first time, I notice how it's very quiet
here in First Class. I drain the brandy, listening to the *hum hum*
of the cabin lights against my gulps. Below us, Las Vegas
is an orange watchglass someone shattered. I think
about the neon people down there, the funny cowboy with tubes
of brown light for a ten-gallon hat, & I think how hard it must be
to make brown neon, & how we still need science.

After a moment, I feel Redford take the snifter
from my hand. He lowers it into the circular depression
in his tray. The plastic hazes where my palm
has touched. Redford reaches over, snapping
my tray into the seatback. Then he finds the place
where my safety belt catches. He gently pulls until
the belt tightens, low & quiet on my hips. He keeps his palm
on the buckle & I settle back. What made me, made me.
Above our heads the reading lights go out.

AFRO

Whereas these strands, well-oiled & diligent in their parts, & appearing in tensile character an iron cloud-net several times the diameter of the head—these strands have I in passing conduct, fidelity, & stewardship, in all protein & mineral accompaniments, in darkness of kerchief & darkness of hands, these have I spirited across the snow & the American seas, from thence to plinths & palettes opportune for discharge of this trust—these strands, which rest in trust to me & which I have dragged a small way into this Country, seeking & halting, desirous to prevent mishap, the undue severance of charge, the tease, the crop & bang, desirous only of those victuals which may furniture my constant guard—whereas for this have I gainsaid the touch of free-booter, the tang of sea-rover & divers others—drinkers, tinkers, kings & clothiers all. These strands, wherein silence bides, close as horses in an afternoon of rain, these ropes which rise against containment & the blur of slang, for these do I come forth in torrents, do I come forth in tenderness & earth do I come forth in rage *for these, for these.*

VALENTINE

Suppose it was a cold throwdown for my affection.
Who would win, Jack White or Jack Black?

You have to think in three dimensions here:
Jack White, Jack Black, & one acoustic guitar.

I'm the fourth dimension in a yellow wig & small purse.
OK, let's have a ref.

I choose Senator Patrick Leahy, Democrat, of Vermont.
We all gather at the bar: *Hi, Ref.*
We all get free No. 2 pencils from Vermont.
Vermont is rad.

Then we see a mini throwing-star. It's zipping over us.
It's Jack Black's.

Intense I say. Jack White opens his shirt. He takes out
some kind of raptor. *This is totally poisonous* he tells me.
Cool I tell him.

*It'd be pretty cool to win this fight for you.
I mean, throwdown* he says.

The poisonous raptor spits onto the floor.
Jack White isn't hot, exactly.

Another mini throwing-star goes by.
I decide to stand behind the bar.

Bartender says: *Little darlin' that is some doggone wig.*
Come on & get you some Grainbelt.

We drink our Grainbelts.
We watch the raptor dig a hole in Jack Black's neck.

Now he's stacking mini throwing-stars inside.
Bartender says: *Moves secretary-like.*

Sure does I say. I bet you can't speak too well
with a neck full of blades.
I'm not sure, but I'm pretty sure.

Once, I saw the moon.

TURN BACK YOUR HEAD & THERE IS THE SHORE

Not by sailfish alone shall the eater live. This morning, she shuts herself in the galley & uses a flat knife to plate her own tongue in white fondant. This new tongue far surpasses the old: ballast-heavy & warm against the teeth. The bridge deck of her mouth buckles down with it. The eater feels like a music-box tune, weepful & thin. She is whittling down, as they say. Smiling out from darkness. Someone has decorated this whole entire ballroom with fairy lights, & it's summer now on the salt-planked sea. The eater descends a spiral staircase, tugging off one satin glove. How easeful it is below. *When lights go out, experiments go on* says the captain, bowing from his glimmering waist. His face resembles the wood of the pear tree. The eater threads her bare forearm through the crook of his elbow. Together they listen to the cellists drawing their bows across marzipan cellos. A kiss before midnight is all it will take to turn the eater into foam. In the ocean, there are no window seats, no aisles, no seats together, no bulkhead seats, no seats.

19: What is the last song that was stuck in your head?

A song I heard coming from a car window this morning. I don't know its name.

"Acorns and Orioles," Guided by Voices

"Amazing Grace"

"Babylon System," Bob Marley

"Big Pimpin'," Jay-Z

"Billie Jean," Michael Jackson

"Black Hand," Cadence Weapon

"Bring it on Home to Me," Sam Cooke

"Can't Keep Johnny Down," They Might be Giants

"Commissioning a Symphony in C," Cake

"Dancing in the Dark," Bruce Springsteen

"Encourage Yourself," Donald Lawrence & the Tri-City Singers

"Happy Birthday to You"

"Hey Hey My My," Neil Young

"Holiday in Cambodia," The Dead Kennedys

"I Don't Like," remix of Chief Keef

"If You Want to Sing Out, Sing Out,"

Incy Wincy Spider

"Knockin' on Heaven's Door"

"Last Christmas," Wham

"Lost and Found," Lianne La Havas

"Love is Blindness," Jack White cover of U2

"Make Room on the Mantle for Your Trophy," made up

"Mama, You Been on My Mind," Bob Dylan

"Mid-Air," Paul Buchanan

"More Bounce to the Ounce," Zapp

"Northern Lights," Kate Boy

"Patches," Clarence Carter

"Put on a Happy Face," Dick Van Dyke

"Ritual Union," Little Dragon

"Sex," The 1975

Some ballad from *Les Misérables*

Star Wars Theme

"The Please Front," Daniel Figgis

"Third Stone from the Sun," Jimi Hendrix

"Turn Off the Radio," Dead Prez

"Unsatisfied," Replacements

"Wake Up," Arcade Fire

"Who Says," Selena Gomez

"You Can't Rollerskate in a Buffalo Herd," Roger Miller

ZACH SAVICH is the author of three books of poetry, including *The Firestorm*, and a book of prose, *Events Film Cannot Withstand*, published by Rescue Press in 2011. He teaches at the University of the Arts in Philadelphia and serves as an editor with *The Kenyon Review*.

SERENADE

In the painting by Degas, the dancer is not
on a cell phone, but holding her head. I left the museum.
Ann was sick. There were shoes all along the bridge,
and the senseless branching of ambulance sirens: one going west
on Henderson, another east. Technicolor weather. A man
in white coveralls was carrying a traffic cone
over his head, he was an Elmer's glue tube.
In the painting of terns on rigging,
when you remove the terns from the rigging, there is
only canvas behind, not sky. Ann vomited
off the bridge, the way a single page can slide
from its binding. It became harder for me to read on
in the biography, knowing there is no part of the body
a bullet hasn't pierced. Piercework. I worked in a chowder house
and got to bring home all the innards we extracted
from bread bowls. I had a friend who was a trumpet player
who'd come home from a show and, sleepless, play more.
His apartment was so small, his trumpet
stuck into the alley. Ann slept for two or three months.
Snow like tissue after tissue pulled from a box.
I drove Ann to the hospital. On the first day of spring I saw
the Elmer's man standing on the traffic cone point
of his head at a rave. Trees blossomed outside the hospital
the way champagne bottles christen ships. I wheeled Ann
to the museum and we watched the Indian out front
raise his arms to weather. I talked about the Caravaggios
facing each other in Santa Maria del Popolo, the pose
of Paul, receiving, so close to the pose of Peter,
received; saints open their arms. Pieced through.
My friend the trumpet player emptied his spit valve onto pigeons.
He watched a woman climb onto her fire escape, nude,

her husband cursing from the window. I gave up on
the biography. I left the rave. Ann held her head.
The ambulances were just roaming, moving things around.
I put on some shoes I found on the bridge, then left the bridge.
Ann bruised. Her mom showed up. It was July.

I SUPPOSE I DO BELIEVE IN NOTHING

I suppose I do believe in nothing / the live thing brown
in a bright bush: earthy swallows / and loneliness, a rain
washed-out wanted poster / can't our solution be
it's not a problem? / pyrocumulous: the forest fire
conducts its own weathered system / electric razor smelling
of an old camera and white floral room at the
rear of a dank church this priest goes brightly to / the tears
are wax / candles warmed by hand which preserves
the wick much as you might think the soul / at the library
she stamps each inside page and I feel similarly marked /
they removed everything they could from the eunuch thinking
it might make his song ever more pure

THE EYE IS THE SEXIEST THING TO LOOK AT

I've dismantled the ladder and nailed its scraps
directly to an elm. This is how the first swimmers
must have felt: I dreamed you swam out past
the rocks, and swam out. I've tried to see the gardener
leaning against the railing as leaning against the raining.
The leaves go orange like a hole opening
in the knee of my jeans. The leaves break
into a single leaf. Bells in the square: no pattern,
just time. In the silent film, we measure the volume
of a flowerpot's crash by how many pieces it breaks into.
We measure the volume of a lion's roar
by how fast the villagers run. And if the villagers continue
to process dyes in their earthen bowls? The lion
is silent or internal. It was once enough to look out windows.
A small iron grill placed in front of any window
turned the room into a balcony. In all the world
there was only a single window divided by walls
and rooms and streets and things. Familiar letting-drop-
a-bicycle-on-the-front-walk motion. Or to again
be carrying a bottle of wine to. Hands passing
among passing trays. There was once a look given in reply;
the look was a given. (Drawbridge splits, sail curtains
through, a boy throws an apple core at the uncurtailable
hound.)

20: What's the last poem that made you laugh, cry or read out loud to someone else?

"A Goddamn Magic Show," Dana Ward

"A Hearing," Robyn Schiff

"Age," Kay Ryan

"An Unsuccessful Play," Daniil Kharms

"Bite Me," Beth Ann Fennelly

Brecht's description of Margarete
Steffin's traveling objects

"Brooklyn Bridge,"
Vladimir Mayakovsky

Emily Dickinson's Master Letters

"Esthétique du Mal," Wallace Stevens

"Everything I Learned About
Jazz I Learned From Kenny G.,"
Marcus Wicker

"G-9," Tim Dlugos

"Gone for the Day, She Is the Day,"
Christian Wiman

"Home Remedy," Franz Wright

"How to Survive a Hotel Fire,"
Angela Veronica Wong

"The Iliad," Homer

I don't know but I wish it was a
poem called SEAWEED SALAD

"In Heaven," Matthew Dickman

"In the Loop," Bob Hicok

"It's So Easy," Dana Ward

"Jenny Kiss'd Me," Leigh Hunt

"Key Episodes from an
Earthly Life," CD Wright

"Man with a Grasshopper
on His Nose," Selima Hill

Martial's Epigrams

"Memorial," Alice Oswald

"moonchild," Lucille Clifton

"Ode to Hoisting," Paula Cisewski

"Old Lem," Sterling A. Brown

"On an East Wind from
the Wars," Alan Dugan

"Palm Trees," Nick Twemlow

"Pecked to Death by Swans,"
Thomas Lux

"Saint Judas," James Wright

"Temple Near Quang Tri, Not
on the Map," Bruce Weigl

"The Drag Queen Dies in
New Castle," Bruce Snider

"This Solitude of Cataracts,"
Wallace Stevens

"To Sustain Distress," Mathias Svalina

Some poems in *Strike
Anywhere*, Dean Young

"Ventriloquy," Hsia Yü

"You Are a Prince,"
Gretchen Primack

ROBYN SCHIFF is the author of *Worth* (2002) and *Revolver* (2008), both published by the University of Iowa Press. She is a co-editor at Canarium Books and teaches poetry at the University of Iowa.

H1N1

God knows how our neighbors manage to breathe.
No one is allowed
to touch me

for infection is a hazard of mercy
I will not transmit
as Legion transcribed from the mouth

of Error into his body
and sent into a herd of swine
who sent it to the sea

who's been trying to return
to earth since creation
and nearly succeeds every day.

I just took my temperature.
98 degrees. I am better than healthy.
I am cooling even as the earth

heats, even as it meets the sea
further inland and negotiates
distance from increasingly

disadvantaged position. I
am cooling because nothing
touches me.

Others may go to the petting zoo
and country fair
but don't even tell me what they touch

there. I'm taking my temperature again;
my thermometer is digital and pink
and its beep is my name

being read from the book of life,
which is available on Kindle
and allows me to avoid the public library

but contains peculiar punctuation
errors and is transcribed by
evangelists while they wait

in line at gates you can't see from here. 98.5.
Still cooler than life. I have another
glass of water, and feel you turning in me,

my little book, flipping over and over,
it's time for bed little sow, little sow.
The book of death is open on my bedside

table and is called *The Pregnancy
Countdown,* and contains "advice from the
trenches" about how to level

the enemy the body.
It's time for bed, little bee, little bee. I open my window
and find ten dead between the pane and the screen

which apparently has tears big enough
to enter and I leave them in state
in a pile and watch

the wind lift their
mighty wings in deathly
aspiration. It is the beginning

of flu season, Rosh Hashanah.
Every tear is recorded. I say tear
to rhyme with the chair by my window,

not tear to rhyme with the fear of God
here at the Fair of God
where the just

leer at the milk cow
and brush up against
captivity and slaughter

in the name of zoonosis
and the vector. Nothing touches me,
little scale, little scale,

I will not be meted I will
not give the mosquito
her share even though the blood meal

is all she has to nurture her eggs
and mother to mother I hear
her flight even as she's drawn

to my breath by fate and nature,
which are one and as interchangeable
as babies in soap operas. Dangerous angel,

I will not lie down
with the lamb who is
contagious. I will not

hear your name recalled for I
have not named you and fear
tempers my love of the letters

of this world which are as
pins through the body
while the wings flail, but I

will not fail to meet you
when you get here
with your shadow

attached and your
failure a promise
entering the success

of your first breath. On what
grounds, on what faith,
dare we aspire

together where Legion
hears the ventilator
and enters the wire?

MULTI-PURPOSE STEAMSHIP FURNITURE, BY TAYLOR & SONS

is made of patent cork fiber for buoyancy, a room
within a room, life-couch docked confidently in a suite
in which everything else would sink or dissolve into a crypt room
many leagues below, roomy
enough to allow a whole school of mackerel and their natural enemy, the shark, to
    change
direction through catacombs of mouldering china sunk from table settings in
    ballrooms, dinner rooms, tea rooms, and the private bedrooms
of independent travelers of independent means into craggy heaps like the cliff faces
    on which manor houses fall to ruin, indistinguishable—from the distant
    view of the traveler spending
the final twists of journey dwelling in awe on it—from the land itself. In dwelling,
    she both must spend
time contemplating and inhabiting the gloomy walks, the compromised stairs
    opening on room after room
as her life
depends on it, while she in possession of Multi-purpose life-

affirming Steamship Furniture floats from her comparable devastation lively
in the manner she reposed upon it, reading, I suppose, as the first order of
    multi-purposefulness is conversion from couch to bed, sitting room to bedroom
as the whole doubles as life
raft, as life
preserver. Life itself doubles in the face of water. Put a stick in it, you know what I
    mean. Refraction is the one sweet
clue to suggest going back in time, but a moment, or is it forward? you would keep
    your integrity as you plunge into water, but, as it is, life's
series of steppings forward sift short-lived
as through prisms, ever-changing,
as graceful or abrupt as a change
in conversation, depending who's talking. Sometimes life

depends upon the ease of such disgressions, and the energy spent
planning to slip undetected into recesses darker yet, whole nights spent

considering the most likely architecture between two known doors on unlikely ends
    of unexplored ruin, balances with that spent
finally traveling it, but a moment, a spark's life.
Put your hand in water. You divide between two rooms, this and the one light
    hesitates to pass through the border of in which you spend
the afternoon beside yourself, an alternative taking place unperceivably later. Even
    in a lifetime spent
going in and out of water, the lost time doesn't amount to much—it won't add up to
    a few more minutes in the bedroom
with you on a rainy November morning, which is what I'd spend
my border change on were reimbursements made for time lost being refracted and
    refracted almost every time we move through this slow, cheating universe that
    spends
me even as I step closer to you. Let us remember to move between realms indivisibly
    in darkness, as Multi-purpose Steamship Furniture, by Taylor & Sons converts
    swiftly and sweetly
without a light to read by from cabin furniture to life preserver before the wave
    rising beneath the very suite
it occupies fully spends
the force of its crest, which is to say, it changes
unchanged.

Change
not given. Everything valued diminishes. Spent
the whole day reading again, and by the end, had to change
my opinion of what I'd hoped were ghosts changing
the living,
but they changed
suddenly material as if winter passed over the novel and everything numinous
    froze in a quick change

in the weather of mystery. The room
emptied, the room
key turned silently, and the change
in me was complete. Sweet,
sweet

Taylor & Sons, is this any way to save oneself? Opportunist, another name for
    multi-purpose, questions the eponymous sweetness
of the rose, for which I name this changing
stanza "my sweet
one." How will I use the word sweet
again? How will I spend
my light? How will I use the word sweet?
How will I use the word sweet?
How does my life
differ from my life?
How will I use the word sweet?
There is no room
in this life, no life in this room.

**JAMES
SHEA**

is the author of
Star in the Eye,
selected for the
Fence Modern
Poets Series.
His poems have
appeared in
various journals,
including *Boston
Review, Colorado
Review, Denver
Quarterly*, and
The Iowa Review.
He has taught at
the University
of Chicago,
Columbia College
Chicago, DePaul
University, and
as a poet-in-
residence in the
Chicago public
schools. He is an
assistant professor
at Nebraska
Wesleyan
University.

AROUND THE WIND

You are the performance artist
who charges people to leave.

You were having an affair with the sky.
You filmed as much as you could.

I can't imagine any wish without a stain.
There was a shiny animal in the street

that ran at my legs. I called out to it, Ryan.
I get in a plane and look for the earth.

I am without the sight of existence for miles.
I can see nothing from all sides.

Do you hear that plane in the sky?
It sounds like the motor went out.

There was heavy heavy snow. Time passed by.
I would land a plane on your street.

HAIKU

Upon Kissing You After You Vomited.
Upon Walking You Home and You Pissing
in Your Pants. Upon Asking a Complete Stranger
about Our Situation. Upon Reading Issa's
Prescripts "Issa in a State of Illness,"
"At Being Bewildered on Waking" and Realizing
the Haiku Poets Were Not So Laconic and How
Could They Be? Poem Before Dying. Poem
Shortly Before I Head to Dinner. Poem in Which
I Enter Drops of Dew Like a Man with Tiny Keys.
Hitomaro has a poem called On Seeing
the Body of a Man Lying Among the Stones
on the Island of Samine in Sanuki Province.
Kanyu's short poem is called A Poem
Shown to My Niece Sonshō on Reaching
the Barrier of the Ran After Being Relegated
to an Inferior Position. Poem Louis Aragon
Would Be Proud Of. Poem I'll Never Show You.
Poem Written in a Bugs Bunny Cartoon as the
Plane's Controls Come Off in My Hands. Poem
that Jerks Around Like a Hamster in a Bag. Bashō
wrote a haiku for his students that he claimed
was his death poem. The night before
he said that for the last 20 years every poem
he had written had been his death poem. Upon
No Longer Recalling My Thoughts When I Was a Boy
Within My Father's Stare. At Being Exhausted
at Having to Explain Why Using Slang
Is More Fun Than Reading a Dictionary of Slang.
The poet Saikaku once wrote 23,500 verses

in 24 hours. Bashō saw Mt. Nikkō and said,
"I was filled with such awe that I hesitated
to write a poem." Upon Looking Past You
into the Mattress, into the Faces of Prior Lovers.
Upon Trying to Cultivate My Inner Life While
also Killing My Ego. On Watching
a 200 pd. Endangered Orangutan
Rape My Wife While She Shouts at Me
Not to Shoot Him. On Seeing a Bloodshot
Spanish Boy Who Was Not Even Crying He Was So Sad
and Not Even Crying He Was So Sad. Poem
in Which I Embody a Moment So Vividly, So
Succinctly, Yet Decorate It with Such Sills,
Such Elaborations. Upon Doodling Your Name
Which Became Your Face Emerging From Day-Old
Coals. Upon Reading that Bashō Believed "A Haiku
Revealing 70 to 80% of Its Subject Is Good, Yet
Those Revealing 50 to 60% Will Never Bore Us."
On Finally Leaving My Attic and Hearing English
for the First Time in 20 Years and It Sounding
Like an Animal's Cry Before It Attacks. Poem
in Response to Flying all the Way to Rome
to Meet You and Being Dumped at the Airport.
Poem about the Next Two Weeks We Spent Together.
Poem as I Sit on This Curb with My Head
in My Hands. Poem After Learning the Japanese
Word for the Simultaneous Feeling of Love
and Hatred. Poem for the Mountain at the End
of My Street. Poem in Response to Some of My
Recent Poems that Seem to Have Been Written
Inside an Aquarium. On Spending a Week in Silence
at a Monastery and Not Being Allowed Pen or Paper.

On Meditating and Feeling Like I Was a Blue Flame.
On Getting Up and Scribbling Something in the Bathroom.
On Stopping at the Train Tracks and Having a Deer
Break His Head Through My Passenger Window,
Stare at Me, and Then Run Back into the Wood.

UNPERFECTABLE

As you suggested, the beauty
of the house amazed me. It was sleeting now.
But that was okay. The trees
had already prepared for winter.

From then on I wanted advice daily.
I thought I missed the quarter-
colored sky and felt restricted
by a natural, beautiful event.
But it was semi-logical
you said. Like a mystery
I knew how to perceive.

You showed me how when
a storm comes it belongs to everyone.
And when we met, we drank
immediately. In the same sense,
you said yellow is the color of sunflowers,
sunflowers equal summer and summer
equals freedom from troubles.

Later my son said, Hey, you pain me.
My heart is a discrepancy. And I
left for your house and you said
how you wouldn't really say that.
How we draw ourselves back like strings.
My new life needs a new death.
How I keep a little of this one left.

NICK TWEMLOW'S first book, *Palm Trees*, published by Green Lantern Press, won the Norma Farber First Book Award from the Poetry Society of America. He is a senior editor of *The Iowa Review* and co-edits Canarium Books. Twemlow's film and video works have played Tribeca, SXSW, Slamdance, and other film festivals. He is a recipient of a Princess Grace Foundation Honorarium in Filmmaking. He teaches poetry and film at Coe College.

I LOVE KARATE

I love karate. I love karate so much I sweat karate steak dinners. I love karate so much I eat karate cereal in the morning, karate sandwiches for lunch, and karate haiku for pleasure. But like a good karateka (that's the technical term for highly skilled karate person) I don't eat karate dessert. You know why? Because dessert takes the edge off. You might ask, Off what? but if you do, I'll perform a random karate move on you, as I did my mother when she tried to serve me non-karate cereal, one morning. That was the morning when I realized that I was a true karateka. I refused the Empire's cereal. If you are a true karateka, you are a rogue. Rogues don't like the Empire. This means that rogues spend a lot of time building dojos in the woods. A dojo is the technical name for a rogue who spends a lot of time building cabins in the woods. There are some karate moves that I can't show you. Those are secret karate moves. Like all karate moves, they are designed to kill. But these secret strikes kill faster and harder. They are to regular karate moves what hardcore is to softcore pornography. I was sensitive once, but karate got rid of that. Now, I am tough on the inside as well as the outside. For example, if I was in the Oval Office partying with the President, smoking some grass (which I'd fake doing because karatekas don't smoke grass) I'd ask him to repeat what he said about kicking evil's ass and then I'd ask him to show me how he'd do it. Since I know the President isn't a karateka, I'd administer a very secret strike on him at the moment he showed me how he'd do it. That's pretty much how I'd do things. I want karate to be in the Olympics in Beijing because I want to be on the team and travel to Beijing and win a gold medal. Or at least that's what I'd trick everyone into thinking I was doing. Part of being a good karateka means bolstering the Chinese economy. Sort of like ninjas except a karateka can beat a ninja fourteen out of ten times. So while people would think I wanted to go to Beijing to win a gold medal and hang out in the Olympic Village and have a really good time with all the other athletes and media and officials and tourists, I'd really have a secret agenda. Secret agendas are pretty common for most karatekas. Secret agendas ensure that no matter what you say, you really don't mean it. So when everyone else was having a good time at the Olympics in Beijing, seeing how Communism is really good on the citizens of China because the government rounded up, the year before, tens of thousands of homeless people and relocated them to work details in provincial labor camps, I'd slip out at night and administer random karate moves on officials of the Empire. This happened a lot in Atlanta, too, when we held the Olympics. The part about the homeless, I mean.

I HATE KARATE

I see you seeing me. I wonder wonder wonder what will become of you. I hate that I
hate, but alas, I still hate. I seethe. Karate can go fuck itself. Can kill itself. Can fight
itself to the death. That's what karate does. It's all about ratings. I hate ratings. I
hate ratings so much I develop my own reality show. In this show, you, viewer, are
asked to watch me hate. I'll hate anything. But I'll hate karate first and foremost. I
hate karate when I'm strung out and panhandling on the corner where I grew up
and happy to accept a farthing. I hate karate when my credit card is declined and
I've got formula and diapers and wipes and a baby that hasn't stopped crying since
I was born. I am a master of the hate. I'll hate anything you present to me. Robert
Creeley? Hate him. My cancer-stricken mother. Hate her. Your photos of your
child, the delicate balance you maintain between love and work. Dress me up in
a suit made of hate, stitched together by ten-year-old Indonesian children. Then,
watch me hate them, their piety, and their sleepless nights, their fingers worked to
the bone. I hate Steve Jobs. He hate me? Then there's enough hate in this world to
keep it spinning. Like a dreidel made of razor blades. I'll give one to my son on the
first day of Hanukkah, and tell him that when he sees blood, it's just the color of all
those who have hated you since you first walked the earth. You, destined to wander
and negotiate, grovel, plead, and every other mode of humiliation that can be im-
agined. Because, my son, you have been hated on since your God asked Abraham
to make the ultimate sacrifice. This Christmas season, when I sit you on Santa's
fat and happy lap, give him this dreidel. Better: Shove it in his mouth and tell him
to bite down hard. When he bleeds his hate, tell him you were sent to purify his
soul, his pitiless, black soul filled with lumps of coal, themselves the very essence
of hate. Don't hate the hater, my son. The hand that spins the dreidel comes from
above. It is the hand of hate. It is your salvation.

TOPEKA, TOPEKA

Topeka, half the moon is rotten with shadows pooling in the Sea of Topeka.

Topeka, where first I wet my brain with a 40oz bottle of Topeka.

Topeka, is place name, is damn shame, is a mirror made of sand & Topeka.

Topeka, you are substandard. I am not. Yet I'm the one on my hands & knees, search-
    ing for the lost keys in the prairie grass, ripped on acid, loving the fallacy that
    the black keys equal melancholy, the black keys being Topeka.

Topeka, miscast capital, you're no more political than a handshake with your dream-
    self upon waking, in my case dream-self lives & dies in Topeka.

Topeka, the sickness cannot be cured of Topeka.

Topeka, tigers laze about the yards, a man with a box balanced on his head, his
    possessions stuffed to brimming, trots down Topeka Ave.

Topeka, the sickness will go unnoticed. The vaccine is composed of rare
    sentiments, the kind that love & hate with equal abandon, love & hate,
    love & hate, love & hate. Topeka.

Topeka, there was a night when the moon didn't appear but it appeared everywhere else
    in the world, what happened that night? Topeka?

Topeka, I fear for your life, the intersection of 29th & California is a portal to Hell. I died
    there twenty times in my youth. Today, driving through, I toss a bouquet
    of roses to mark my third death, the one that had a soundtrack I can't shake free.
    My sister sings it from the shower every morning. Forecast calls for
    occasional showers, with the possibility of late-morning sleet, in Topeka.

Topeka, cast off the reliquaries! Call your men to war! Me? I'll be tugging one last hit
    from the bong I fashioned out of the shrapnel of Topeka.

Topeka, pop. rarely exceeds one, as in each trip home happens in rewind, stepping back
    across the creek, bird in hand throwing up the worm, further back, unbreaking
    its wing, bird flying off as if resurrected but from among the living, there
    I am, eight years old, seven, six, now a slug of semen sucked back into my
    father, now, as the waters roll back across the plains toward the river, a dog
    coughs up water, lifts its head, sees nothing, puts its head back down, this,
    Topeka, is your history, although it never happened.

EMINENT VICTORIANA

So I walk into the house Mies van der Roe
designed at gunpoint, the cocaine was tiresome
by this point, but that was its attraction.
I can take anything I want because I have been filmed
fucking the richest heiress in the known world.
I would like the word you keep locked
in the safe behind the Richter in the guest bedroom.
The word for the kind of ease that you recline
into after a colonic and tonic.
Give me supersonic. I want the gardener's
daughter's virginity, the fall
of Rome and the rise
of a gangster nation. I fucked everything.
I fucked the Cornish game hen.
It was so lifeless I put a fork in its face.
I am too young to remark on death.
I hope it resembles the view
you tear open
with your toy sword, toy sword,
say it ten times fast.

**SARAH
VAP**

is the author of
five collections
of poetry. The
most recent
are *Arco Iris*
(Saturnalia
Books), which
was named a
Library Journal
Book Best Book
of 2012 and *End
of the Senti-
mental Journey*
(Noemi Press,
2013). She is a
recipient of a
2013 National
Endowment of
the Arts Grant
for Literature.

COLD RED TILES. RED-HOT BATH.

Hallucination
when I come: Imposters

moving through the desert, and up to the mouth of the world.

We are bent, early and late, and let ourselves be. And hate to death

the nursing dog
who crawled to us near the river—like hedges, the deer.

–

Beach: unrest. *Rest*. A waiting-room full of housekeepers who are
buying, rebuying

what is smoothed away. Who call out underwater,
and now it happens:

the world has an eye. It watches the people drown.
Its nose

          red with pleasure. Its little dogs crazy.

–

At least five signs. Your tongue curls, then freezes
when you yawn. You say *Please, no*. And then *believe me*.

How many times I won't be there—da da da da da
what ends by making.

MY ATTENTION

deficit disorder—originality
about myself no matter what. It happened a little bit later
when I found someone to love. I have
a really sarcastic thing to say about the beginnings
of sincerity—get away
from the original as soon as possible like any
ordinary woman, systematic
with my DNA-cake. The longstanding questions of my life: I called dolls
child as a child—my desire
to lift strangers up. Accompanied
by inarticulation, and details of the genius
that would extend my attention.

QUICKENING

I anticipate, as stallions anticipate—our work.
Toward a horse-faced river, horseflies—or the sounds
of children at play

as countless horses in the river—

we both know
how to heed a calling. We both know

what patience is—it rips out your throat—.

JERRY WILLIAMS'S
first collection of poems, *Casino of the Sun*, published by Carnegie Mellon University Press in 2003, was a finalist for the Kate Tufts Discovery Award. His second collection, *Admission*, published by Carnegie Mellon in 2010, received the Devil's Kitchen Reading Award. In addition, he served as editor of the anthology, *It's Not You, It's Me: The Poetry of Breakup*, published by The Overlook Press in 2010. His poetry and nonfiction have appeared in *American Poetry Review, Tin House, New Ohio Review, Pleiades, Witness,* and many other literary journals. He lives in New York and teaches creative writing at Marymount Manhattan College.

CASINO OF THE SUN

It's Christmas day in Arizona:
one hundred and sixty degrees above zero and rising.
When you get off the plane,
which you secretly hoped would crash,
and pass through that gray chute,
your old roommate, the Chin, greets you,
lathered in the ocher of a different time zone.
Nakedly joyful, a boy of ten or eleven
jumps into his father's arms.
A camera flashes and the Chin snorts,
Another chat room dream come true.
Close your eyes, imagine giving birth
to a thousand mallard ducks inside a shark cage
while some non-union uniform runs a metal detector
up and down your leg, up and down your other leg.
Welcome to hell. Try not to spill your margarita.
Try not to let the molten parking lot solidify
in your lungs when you hear about your ex-girlfriends
riding the cranks of hard-minded day traders
in Mustique or Minorca
or wherever people go who have parents.
There's a bed waiting for you in the desert,
though the sheets were not prepared for your arrival.
The cordless phone is dead,
but the cable television works fine.
Shaquille O'Neal just missed another free throw,
and we all know why. He brings the ball
too close to his face; he smells his fingers.
He's distracted by his own good fortune.
Those guys have it made: ballplayers.
The Chin says they live like dolphins.

Shaq, Sprewell, Allen Iverson. Sweet.
What am I doing here anyway? This is not my affair.
I've drunk blood from a leopard print purse,
said *I love you* under my breath,
shared an apartment with a terrified and weeping,
uprooted fleshpot
who caught me looking at pictures of lepers.
I have checked the pulses of dead husbands
and disagreed with the diagnosis,
listened through walls for signs of forgiveness,
been counted on and let down and squeezed out.
I bet I would sell my organs in China,
I would build electric chairs for a dollar an hour
if I could only put together enough scratch
to go back in time and burn the right bridges.
By next Christmas, I vow to pledge my life and mind,
my entire troubled essence,
to a beautiful cyborg with reliable taxonomy
and skin the color of grape soda.
But for now, the Chin toasts the end of an era
in a bar on the edge of effectiveness.
A lonely jingle leaks out of the sound system,
and the patrons sing along like there's no tomorrow.
Every Sunday morning they wake up
with inexplicable cuts and scrapes on their hands.
These are your people.
They would offer you the world
if they had any right to it.

ADMISSION

If an artist becomes too idealistic, he will commit suicide, because between his ideal
and his actual ability there is a great gap. Because there is no bridge long enough to
go across the gap, he will begin to despair. That is the usual spiritual way.
—Shunryu Suzuki, from *Zen Mind, Beginner's Mind* ⸂

An autumn shadow draws across my room.
This morning's remedy hasn't yet kicked in.
I'm losing the bookshelf wars.
Not to a doctor, but to a dream horizon
dotted with enormous nylon sacks
of arrogance and longing and gloom-fueled sloth.
I wanted more. There it is.
I wanted so much more to issue forth.
Wrong or right, I wanted to walk under a bridge
wearing a hat made of prose
and sing Buddy Holly songs in Russian.
I wanted to sell fire and sirens door to door.
Forget the stamen and the pistil.
I wanted a soy toy. I wanted more.
I could eat the breeze right off the curtains.
I wanted to get to the point where what I'm allowed
actually feels like what I desire.
Maybe I should have married A, B, C, D, E, F, G,
and all the rest, but I had to child-proof my entire future,
stand on the roof with a shotgun diploma,
and campaign for National Verb Month.
I wanted to arrive at a different concourse.
I wanted the perfect outlet
for whatever coal dust I might cough up.
I wanted exploits, vehemence, divergence,
characters screaming at each other on stage,
slicing off fingers and chucking them

into the prop sink and then laughing their guts out,
doubled over, tears streaming down their faces,
guffawing, blood up and down their forearms,
gravel and pulverized antiquities underfoot.
No big deal. No human pyramids.
I wanted to love someone so hard
she would never forgive me.
I wanted to rob a bank with a golf club.
I expected more from myself.
I wish I heard voices.
I wish piñatas were filled with naked students and Vicodin.
I thought I would be the scariest mummy
in the museum by now,
but all I am is preparedness,
the implements of my sterility laid out in the dusk.
This here: This is not even what I wanted to say.
I've failed at reverse prayer,
failed to really understand my own eyes.
It's getting dark and I can hear my neighbors creaking.
They must hide the pigeons at night.
My greatest fear is that the love of my life
will be the one who pushes the needle,
the one who tells me to start counting backwards
from forever.

FLYING UNITED

Whenever I'm feeling low I like to hop a flight to Vegas
on the airline whose aptly gray planes are the easiest
to hijack and dive-bomb into the World Trade Center and the Pentagon.
I'm not talking about the T-word; I'm talking about taking
advantage of a situation; I'm talking about economy.
And I don't care whether or not James Dickey actually came up
with "fly the friendly skies" when he worked as an ad man in Chicago.
This silly factoid has been stuck to my recollection for so long
the halituous ramblings of a thousand false martyrs couldn't *burn* it off.
Poor James Dickey, so unfortunately named and a posthumous liar to boot.
The skies are anything but friendly.
For instance:
My sister's a mechanic for the aforementioned bombardier
and now will never see the retroactive cost of living raise
the company promised her union ten years ago.
"Labor *Jihad!*" I advised her in an e-mail transmission—
just before AOL Time Warner Nabisco Pfizer cut off my internet access.
So I'm sitting on this 757, knocking back a Xanax,
and an Arab couple slips down the aisle with their teenage son.
All three are wearing New York Yankees caps
and they have this look in their eyes like every single
white person on the plane has explosives strapped to their chest.
I want to help these people
stow their suitcases in the overhead compartment.
I want to gather their dark portrayals unto my bosom.
But I feel an amateur historian's fugue coming on:
Osama bin Carter, Osama bin Reagan, Osama bin Bush,
Osama bin Clinton, Osama bin Junior, Osama bin Spielberg,
Osama bin Rumsfeld, Osama bin Albright, Osama bin Zeta-Jones,
Osama Cat Stevens, Osama bin Kissinger, Osama bin Hitchens.
By the time the plane reaches altitude, I've implicated everyone

from Euclid to the Dallas Cowboy cheerleaders.

It's too simple to simply blame the enemy.

Culpability is an airborne bio-toxin that nation-states inhale through the eyes;

it smells like fuel oil and forward motion.

Consider the case of young Bob McIlvaine, twenty-six years old, perished, extinguished,

murdered, unplugged, wasted, abolished, man-slaughtered, collaterally damaged.

And for what? Nine hundred years of history? Nobody deserves that.

He stumbled out of the South Tower and crossed Liberty Street,

only to be put out of his happiness by falling debris,

his penultimate thought *I made it* and not *Fuck, that's hot*

or

I wonder if I'll black out before I hit the ground.

At least his loving parents can keep that in mind when they're

funding scholarships and weeping phosphorescently in front of Congress.

Not so suddenly, the seatbelt light goes pong

and the aircraft banks into a turn, begins its descent.

Every head in the cabin chants, *What-if-what-if-what-if*?

I slide my plastic window shade up and a spritz

of desert light lands on the empty seat beside me.

This might be completely irrelevant, but I was in love once.

She was fifteen and I was sixteen.

For elocutionary purposes, I'll call her the Scar. *E pluribus unum.*

I think she peed her pants the first time we made out

in the back of the bus coming home from the Roth game.

A wet spot appeared.

Her Italian-American father, literally, worked in a chocolate factory.

He gargled eight ounces of salt water every morning

and brutalized his children with belts, deprivation, and the palm of his hand.

I wanted to be the *man*, to figure out a way to protect my little ruination,

so I reported the coward to Social Services.

A heavyset woman with no briefcase showed up at their house

and spoke to the family in the living room, surrounded by cream-colored

doilies and crucifixes and pictures of saints with rosaries draped around the frames.

The minute she walked out the door,
Scar said her father slapped her younger brother across the face.
Now I'm wondering what might have happened that could have changed things—
negotiation, apology, more firepower, books, cheese, non-involvement.
Remember this if nothing else: My life is based on a true story.
When that landing gear oozes into place and the captain starts his approach
and I look out my window at a three-quarter-sized Eiffel Tower
straddling a parking garage and across the boulevard a giant black pyramid
trolls for gambling addicts in outer space,
I realize, with the voltage of a Taser jab,
that no one in Iraq or Afghanistan or the former Yugoslavia
will ever be privileged enough to go as far into debt as I am.
In an hour, I'll be hunched over a five-dollar table at Binion's,
content to be baffled and alive and patriotically blowing money,
safer in Las Vegas than in a womb.

**JON
WOODWARD'S**
books are
Uncanny Valley
(Cleveland
State Univer-
sity Poetry
Center), *Rain*
(Wave Books),
and *Mister
Goodbye Easter
Island* (Alice
James Books).
He lives in
Quincy, MA
with his wife,
poet and
pianist Oni
Buchanan,
and he works
at the Harvard
Museum of
Comparative
Zoology.

from *RAIN*

whatever it was that tripped
the latch we like actual
mammals run alongside it our
two eyes look in slightly
different directions neither is important

and our tongue is no
pointer either we are thirsty
we ducked in a shit
ditch an hour thought about
drinking it we ran on

and the thing that tripped
the latch ran on beside
us split a ripe cactus
with a glowing knife we
drank and rested and ran

only half of the house
was haunted at the edge
of the non haunted half
was a cold plaster wall
with a red door the

door was about eight feet
tall about four feet wide
maybe three inches thick but
that's just conjecture I don't
know how it sounded when

it was knocked on I
never knocked the red paint
was peeling off in several
places you could see all
the other colored layers underneath

SALAMANDER

The janitor asked me
how to pronounce the creature's name
& I said salamander for him.

He looked at it on the screen
and I looked at him.

Slide your legs into its tail I said.
I can't he said as he did.
Feed your guts there into its cavity

of guts, I can't he said (manifestly untrue
because he did). Mash the thing's
name and yours I said together into

that irreversible hole I know you keep
and he did & it broke over his face

& flowed, water from the earth,
I can't, I can't, he said.

from *UNCANNY VALLEY*

Push the remote button and
The mechanical brayer brays

Lines notated like the previous two
Are repeated (as a pair)
As many times as the reader desires,
From zero to 255, before continuing.

Similar notation, applied to one word only,
Sometimes |drives down the middle of a line.

The better part of a long drive
Is the most important meal of the bray.

The reader reads aloud,
And the driver drives

Ancient desert robots
Ancient desert robots
Robots of ancient device
Robots of ancient device
Sent seven huge trees
Down onto the motorway
Up onto the overpass
Seven trees landed on there
To kill any and all abominations.

Uprooted trees
Need gravity so bad
Need gravity so bad

Or they get nostrils and |eyes confused

And all abominations were in a car accident
You can't make them out from here,
The facial muscles fade out
Over the distance

The face figures out
Of the distance
Leaving featureless mask
Leaving featureless mask

They totaled
Seven cars, seven bodies
Seven mask, seven muscles
Seven trees, fpushed over
Seven trees, on them

ACKNOWLEDGMENTS & PERMISSIONS

Rescue Press and *The New Census* editors would like to thank the poets, magazines, and press-es who helped bring this book into the world. Thanks also to our creative director, Sevy Perez, for his visionary work shaping and designing this collection, and to Lauren Haldeman for the beautiful illustrations. Additional thanks to Fred Courtright for the generosity and guidance. And finally, thanks to Zach Isom and Alyssa Perry, whose intelligence and friendship helped see this book to the finish line.

Carrie Olivia Adams: "Notes Toward a Short Film" is from *Intervening Absence*, copyright © 2009, reprinted with permission of Ahsahta Press and the author.

Eric Baus: "Organs of the Projector" is from *Tuned Droves*, copyright © 2009, reprinted with permission of Octopus Books. "The To Sound" and "Wondering Why Her Skin Feels Like Sand" are from *The To Sound*, copyright © 2004, Verse Press, reprinted with permission of Wave Books and the author.

John Beer: excerpts from "The Waste Land" are from *The Waste Land and Other Poems*, copy-right © 2010, reprinted with permission of Canarium Books and the author.

Nicky Beer: "Avuncularity" and "Provenance" are from *The Diminishing House*, copyright © 2010, reprinted with permission of Carnegie Mellon University Press. "Ad Hominem" origi-nally appeared in *Poetry* and "Black Hole Itinerary" originally appeared in *Gulf Coast*; both reprinted with permission of the author.

Ciaran Berry: "The Parsley Necklace" is from *The Sphere of Birds*, copyright © 2008, reprinted with permission of Southern Illinois University Press. "At Nero's Circus" and "At Ballycon-neely" are printed with permission of the author.

Jericho Brown: "Track 1: Lush Life," "Track 5: Summertime," and "Tin Man" are from *Please*, copyright © 2008, reprinted with permission of New Issues Poetry & Prose.

Emily Kendal Frey: "KAABA/Kiss the Stone" was originally published in *ESQUE* and is reprinted with permission of the author.

Dobby Gibson: "Polar" and "Upon Discovering My Entire Solution to the Attainment of Immortality Erased from the Blackboard Except the Word 'Save'" are from *Polar*, copyright © 2005, reprinted with permission of The Permissions Company, Inc., on behalf of Alice James Books, www.alicejamesbooks.org. "What It Feels Like to Be This Tall" is from *Skirmish*, copyright © 2009, and "Silly String Theory" is from *It Becomes You*, copyright © 2013, both reprinted with permission of The Permissions Company, Inc., on behalf of Graywolf Press, www.graywolfpress.org.

Yona Harvey: "Sound—Part I (Girl with Red Scarf)," "To Describe My Body Walking," and "Mother, Love" are from *Hemming The Water*, copyright © 2013, reprinted with permission of Four Way Books and the author.

Steve Healey: "All Umbrellas Come From Fire" and "Terminal Moraine" are from *10 Mississippi*, copyright © 2010, reprinted with permission of Coffee House Press. "Essay on the Boy We Almost Ran Over," first appeared in *Revolver Magazine* and is reprinted with permission of the author.

Tyehimba Jess: "#1 Coon Songs Must Go" originally appeared in *Callaloo Journal*. "Blind Tom: Two Graves, One Body" and "Twain v. Tom" originally appeared in the *Indiana Review*. All poems reprinted with permission of the author.

Keetje Kuipers: "Bondage Play as a Substitute for Prayer" and "Across a Great Wilderness Without You" are from *Beautiful in the Mouth*, copyright © 2010. "Drought" and "The Keys to the Jail" are from *The Keys to the Jail*, copyright © 2011, 2012. All are reprinted with permission of The Permissions Company, Inc. on behalf of BOA Editions Ltd., www.boaeditions.org.

Nick Lantz: "'Of the Parrat and other birds that can speake'" is from *We Don't Know We Don't Know*, copyright © 2010, reprinted with permission of The Permissions Company, Inc., on behalf of Graywolf Press, www.graywolfpress.org. "Portmanterrorism" and "The Miracle" are from *The Lightning that Strikes the Neighbors' House*, copyright © 2010 by the Regents of the University of Wisconsin System, reprinted with permission of The University of Wisconsin Press. "Mutton" originally appeared in *jubilat* and is reprinted with permission of the author.

LAUREN SHAPIRO's first book of poems, *Easy Math*, was awarded the 2011 Katherine A. Morton Prize. A former acquiring editor at the Yale University Press, she teaches at Carnegie Mellon University.

KEVIN A. GONZÁLEZ is the author of *Cultural Studies* and co-editor of *jubilat*. He lives in Pittsburgh, where he teaches Creative Writing at Carnegie Mellon University.

RESCUE PRESS